"Afoot and light-hearted I take to the open road,
Healthy, free, the world before me,
The long brown path before me leading wherever I choose"
— **Walt Whitman**

- •9 New Parks
- •More Than 100 Major Revisions

The *EXPANDED* Santa Cruz Mountains Trail Book
THIRD EDITION

by Tom Taber

The Oak Valley Press

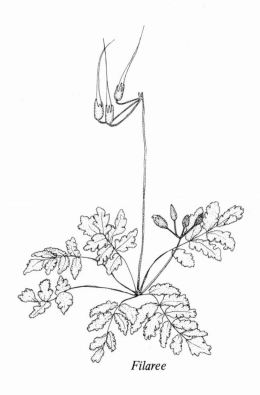

Filaree

PHOTO CREDITS:
Pages 40 and 50 by Charlotte McDonald, courtesy of Midpeninsula
Regional Open Space District. Page 82 by Sempervirens Fund. All
other photographs by Tom Taber.

THE OAK VALLEY PRESS
228 Virginia Ave.,
San Mateo, CA 94402

Table of Contents:

Introduction

When the first edition of *The Santa Cruz Mountains Trail Book* came out in 1976, I wrote that "this book may never be completed." New parks and trails were forming so fast I wondered how I could possibly keep up with all the changes.

My prediction is as true today as it was then; and today this range is one of the Bay Area's most accessible and enjoyable places for walking, camping, backpacking, picnicking, kite flying, nature study, and almost all other kinds of non-destructive outdoor activities.

From its windiest promontories to its darkest and most intimate redwood valleys, the Santa Cruz Mountains invite exploration. So near to the Bay Area, yet so remote in mood, these mountains offer an outstanding system of state, county, and local parks, preserves, and trails traversing all ecological communities.

This book is also about walking, the oldest, and in many ways still the best, means of transportation. People can now travel a lot farther and faster than they used to, but it is doubtful that they see any more of the world than they did when they walked — and probably a lot less.

Recreational walking is an acquired taste — like yogurt. People who have never given it a try think it sounds terrible: sore feet and drudgery; why not ride a dirt bike instead? Actually, walking is easy. Our bodies are designed to get around that way. Walking at a comfortable pace is relaxing and enjoyable. It gives you a chance to see the world in detail, instead of as a blur. It encourages conversation when walking with a companion, and stimulates the mind and senses when going alone. For eons people with great thoughts did their thinking on foot in natural settings. Jesus, Buddha, Darwin, Muir — the list is endless — were all wilderness hikers. Moses didn't jog for forty years through the wilderness — he walked.

This book includes my favorite hiking trails, especially those that exemplify the region's diverse scenic and ecological qualities. My purpose is to describe the parks and trails in order to help hikers decide which they want to explore. It's not my intention to tell you exactly where to turn right and left, where to eat lunch, and when to use the park facilities. There's no adventure in hiking when you know exactly where you are going and what you are going to see when you get there. Honest, folks, the best hiking guides are your feet and your eyes.

Now all you have to do is get a lunch together, find an interesting trail that fits your stamina and time requirements, and go out and learn how to really walk. Lift those feet high, stretch those legs, but don't hike too fast— take your time and enjoy the scenery.

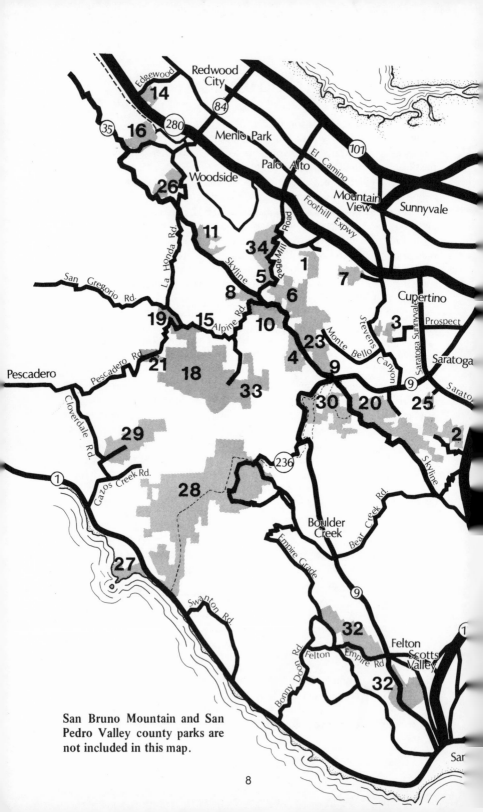

San Bruno Mountain and San
Pedro Valley county parks are
not included in this map.

THE SANTA CRUZ MOUNTAINS VICINITY

OPEN SPACE PRESERVES

1 Duveneck Windmill Pasture
2 El Sereno
3 Fremont Older
4 Long Ridge
5 Los Trancos
6 Monte Bello
7 Rancho San Antonio
8 Russian Ridge
9 Saratoga Gap
10 Skyline Ridge
11 Windy Hill

COUNTY PARKS

12 Almaden Quicksilver
13 Calero Reservoir
14 Edgewood
15 Heritage Grove
16 Huddart
17 Mount Madonna
18 Pescadero Creek
19 Sam McDonald
20 Sanborn Skyline
21 San Mateo Memorial
22 Santa Teresa
23 Skyline
24 Uvas Canyon
25 Villa Montalvo
26 Wunderlich

STATE PARKS

27 Año Nuevo
28 Big Basin Redwoods
29 Butano
30 Castle Rock
31 Forest of Nisene Marks
32 Henry Cowell Redwoods
33 Portola

CITY PARK

34 Foothill Park

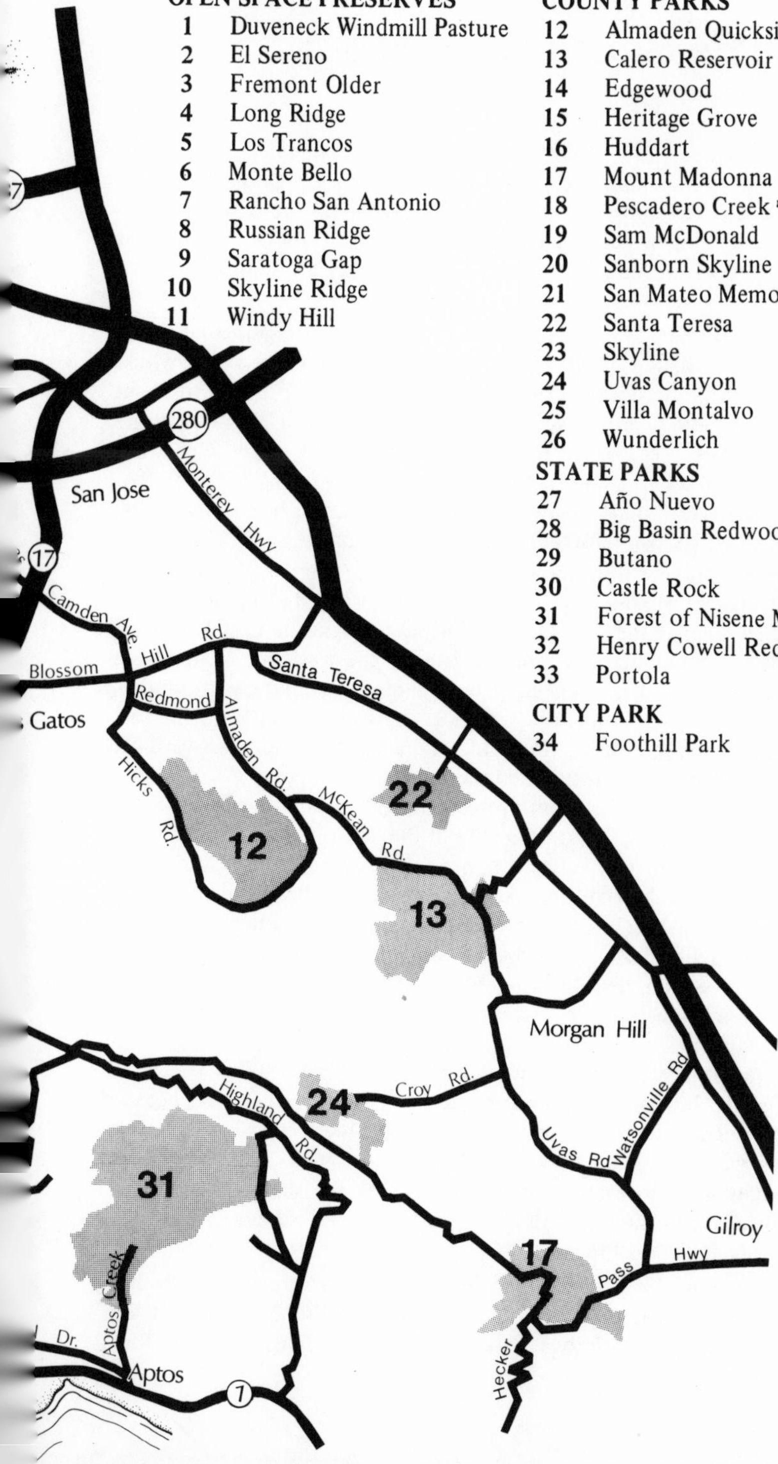

280

San Jose

17

Monterey Hwy

Camden Ave

Hill Rd.

Blossom

Redmond

Gatos

Santa Teresa

Almaden Rd.

Hicks Rd.

McKean Rd.

12

22

13

Morgan Hill

Highland Rd.

Croy Rd.

24

Uvas Rd.

Watsonville Rd.

31

Gilroy

17

Hwy

Pass

Aptos Creek

Dr.

Aptos

1

Hecker

The Santa Cruz Mountains

Geography and Climate

The Santa Cruz Mountains are a range of parallel, northwest-tending ridges extending for about 80 miles from San Bruno Mountain to the Pajaro River. It is narrowest and lowest on the San Francisco peninsula, getting wider, higher, and wilder to the south. The highest peak is 3,800 foot high Loma Prieta, though only a few peaks exceed 3,000 feet.

Deep layers of sedimentary rock, called the Franciscan Formation, were deposited nearly 100 million years ago when this whole area was below the ocean. For incomprehensible ages the land rose and fell. At the time of the Miocene upheavels—about 10 million years ago—it was raised above the sea in northwest-tending ridges as we find it today. Periodic volcanic activity spewed out igneous rock, and to further complicate matters the range was sliced across by several faults, the largest and most famous being the San Andreas.

One of the first things you will notice about the Santa Cruz Mountains is the close relationship between the ocean and the climate. Notice how much greener they are than the Diablo range in the East Bay Area, and how much greener and more forested is the west side of the range than the east side. This range has a coastal marine climate, with rainless summers and greatest moisture—often in the form of fog— on the seaward side of the mountains. Cool, moist marine air sweeps eastward off the ocean and piles up on the mountains' western slopes.

Precipitation varies from more than 40 inches in the Butano and Big Basin area to only about 11 inches in the "rainshadow" in the Santa Clara Valley. Mean maximum summer temperatures range from 70 to 75 degrees fahrenheit during August and September. The minimum temperatures vary from 36 to 40 degrees fahrenheit in January. Snowfall on the higher peaks and ridges is rare and short-lived, and hiking is great in any season. The brown-gold season and the green season each have their own distinct character that adds an appealing diversity to coastal California.

The ideal place for redwoods to grow is away from the brisk ocean winds, but on the seaward side of the range where the coastal fog can cool and dampen the forest. They also like deep, shady canyon bottoms where streams retain moisture all through the dry season. You might also notice that redwoods prefer the shady north-facing slopes where exposure to sunlight is reduced and can't rob the great trees of precious moisture.

During the early spring months a cool air mass called the "Pacific High" gathers north of Hawaii and west of San Francisco. It hits the California coast in a southeasterly course and pushes great quantities of water along the coast. This moist air mass is cooled by contact with deep upwelling water and condenses in the form of fog, which is deflected by the coast range and usually only penetrates the continent at low mountain passes.

Ecology

Notice the relationship between plants and their environment. Oak and madrone are examples of sun-loving trees found on dry ridgetops and on the sunny southside of hills. Chaparral plants such as chamise, sage, manzanita, and scrub oak, grow on the driest parts of the range and are characterized by small leaves and deep roots to conserve moisture. Oak trees are also deep-rooted and have drought-resistant leaves. One of the most noticeable seasonal changes occurs in the grasslands, which change from green to gold as the rains come and go.

Close to 150 species of grasses grow in the Santa Cruz Mountains, though it soon becomes obvious that some species are a lot more common than others. The perennial bunch grasses that once covered these hills have been mostly replaced by the European annuals, which were brought here in the hooves and fur of livestock. The new grasses were so successful they completely changed the character of these hills.

The amazing thing about this herbaceous revolution is that the introduced species were better adapted to survival in California's drought cycle than the natives. The reason for this is that the foreign invaders — the foxtails, fescues, wild oats, and downy chess, to name a few — had several advantages over the bunch grasses: 1) they grow more quickly than the native perennials; 2) they use the winter and spring rainfall more efficiently by growing quickly and then by turning brown to wait out the summer drought.

Notice the fire scars on many old redwoods, evidence of forest fires that swept through the mountains long before Europeans entered the area. Fire actually benefits redwoods by removing competing plants and by exposing minerals soil which is essential to the germination of seedlings. Redwoods are often hollowed out by fire, but their thick and nonresinous bark usually helps them survive and recover. Most redwood reproduction is through sprouting from the roots of existing trees. Notice the kind of plants that cover the redwood forest floor. Ferns, sorrel, wild ginger, and many other beautiful plants thrive in the moist and dark parts of the forest. Notice how sorrel avoids direct sunlight. The leaves lower against the stem — like a butterfly at rest — when struck by sunlight.

California Poppy

Black-tail deer graze on the grassy hillsides; squirrels trapeze across the treetop canopy; steller's jays break the forest calm with their raucous calls; and woodpeckers tap holes in the trees. Banana slugs, those yellow-orange denizens of the creek beds, are among the easiest animals to examine. Pick one up and hold it against the sunlight and wait for the respiratory opening on the right side to open. You can see into the body cavity all the way to the other side.

Other animals you might see include bobcats, skunks, weasels, gray foxes, coyotes, opossums, dusky-footed woodrats, racoons, several species of snakes and lizards, and even mountain lions. Some of these animals are shy when people are around, and you may not see some of them even after years of hiking. Look closely at muddy places along creeks where the pawprints of even the most secretive creatures are often found.

Almaden Quicksilver County Park

TO GET THERE... take Almaden Expressway south to the town of New Almaden. The Mine Hill Trail begins at the dirt road off to the west just north of Alamitos Creek. Or you can take Almaden Expressway south from San Jose, turn west on Camden and south on McAbee to the end of the road.

This roomy 3,570 acre park, with 30 miles of trails, is open exclusively for hikers and equestrians and is a great place to see wildlife.

Turkey vultures often cruise the air currents here, with a sharp eye for anything that might be dead. With a wingspan sometimes exceeding 6 feet, this is one of the Bay Area's largest birds, and can be recognized by their red, naked heads and black feathers. One blistering hot day in September I sprawled out in the shade of a solitary oak on a grassy hillside, maneuvering around for a comfortable position for a short nap. Soon I noticed an inquisitive vulture circling overhead. A few minutes later another one joined the aerial investigation, and by the time a third bird joined the group I lost my desire for sleep. I still wonder how long it takes for a sleeping hiker to be declared dead.

From the Almaden Road entrance, take the Mine Hill Trail uphill for sweeping views as you climb to an altitude exceeding 1,500 feet and then loop back via the Randal Mine Trail. This is an all-day hike with some strenuous grades and passes through grasslands, chaparral, and oak woodlands. From the McAbee Road entrance combine the Mine Hill and Guadalupe trails for an easy hike that loops over a ridge and past Guadalupe Reservoir.

From the McAbee Road trailhead you can walk an easy and scenic 7-mile loop by combining the Mine Hill and Guadalupe trails. Remnants of the quicksilver (mercury) mining that was the base of the local economy are seen. Quicksilver was discovered by Mexican Cavalry captain Andres Castillero in 1845, and this soon became one of the great quicksilver producing areas of the world. As the ore was depleted, however, the thriving mining communities became ghost towns, and the Quicksilver Mining Company declared bankruptcy in 1912.

Situated on the dry east side of the range, the park is covered mostly with oak woods and grasslands, which change from golden brown in summer and autumn to green in the winter and spring. The elevation ranges from less than 400 feet to more than 1,600 feet. If you want to do some rock climbing test your skills on Guadalupe Rock, at the upstream end of Guadalupe Reservoir. During the wet season the base of the rock is often submerged.

This park, only 11 miles south of San Jose, is open from 8 a.m. until sundown. For more information, call the Santa Clara County Parks and Recreation Department at (408) 356-7151.

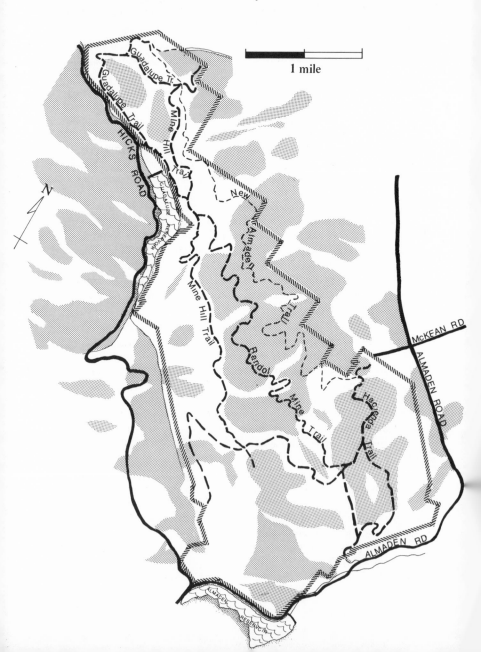

"I think that I cannot preserve my health and spirits, unless I spend four hours a day at least — and it is commonly more than that — sauntering through the woods and over the hills and fields, absolutely free from all worldly engagements."
— Henry David Thoreau

1 mile

Bull elephant seals during breeding season.

Ano Nuevo State Reserve

TO GET THERE . . . take New Years Creek Road off Highway 1 about 19 miles north of Santa Cruz.

Año Nuevo is truly one of America's great marine wildlife preserves.

Cormorants nest on ocean cliffs, tidepools abound with intertidal life, sea lions, fur seals, and harbor seals are commonly seen and heard on the beaches and rocks here, and even sea otters are sited more often every year. But the preserve is most popular from December through March when a colony of elephant seals visits the island and peninsula for mating and bearing young. To protect these enormous mammals, and the people who come to see them, the preserve is open only through naturalist guided tours at this time of the year.

Male elephant seals arrive in December to establish a breeding hierarchy and are followed in January by the females who join the harems of the dominant males. Male seals are enormous, reaching lengths of 16 feet and weighing 3 tons. Females are much smaller, at 1,200 to 2,000 pounds. Slaughtered for their oil-rich blubber, by 1892 less than 100 remained. In the 1920s the Mexican and United States governments gave them legal protection, allowing their numbers to rapidly increase since then. They first returned to Año Nuevo Island in

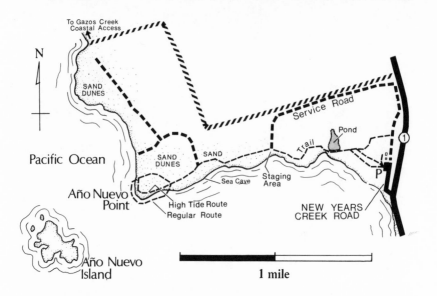

1955 and are now also breeding on the peninsula. These animals, the largest members of the seal family, seem awkward on land, but they are excellent swimmers, able to dive as deep as 1,000 feet to feed mainly on rays, squids, skates, and fish.

This fascinating peninsula is worth exploring all year; and in fact, can be most enjoyable when most of the elephant seals and their hordes of loyal admirers are gone, and walking may be done without ranger escort. Año Nuevo is one of the few places on the San Mateo County coast where it is possible to do some real hiking west from Highway 1.

Follow the trail west from the parking area, passing coastal scrub, a beautiful springtime display of wildflowers, and a small marshy pond. A little over half way to the point a wonderful sea cave invites exploration at low tide for those hardy enough to make their way down the steep embankment. Continue over the dunes and along the beach to the end of the peninsula, which is just over a mile from the parking lot, depending on your route.

Half a mile off the peninsula is 12-acre Año Nuevo Island, breeding ground for elephant seals, California and steller sea lions, and harbor seals, and a nesting place for western gulls, pigeon guillemots, and black oystercatchers. Because of its importance to coastal wildlife, public access to the island is prohibited. This cherty shale island was part of

Park rangers and students from the University of California at Santa Cruz conduct tours of the preserve when elephant seals are here in their greatest numbers between December and March. As of this writing, tickets are available from Ticketron. Because of the popularity of these tours, be sure to get your tickets as early as possible. For more information, call the state parks office at (415) 879-0227.

the mainland until relatively recently in geologic time, when it was separated by wave erosion and by the gradual rising of the sea level when the ice age glaciers melted over the last ten thousand years.

This area was uplifted from the sea a mere 70-100 thousand years ago — practically yesterday to geologists — creating treacherous rocky obstacles for ships. Several major shipwrecks resulted in the construction of a lighthouse on the island in 1890. Difficult to maintain, the storm-battered station was replaced by an automated signal buoy south of the island in 1948. Today, the weathered lightkeepers' house still stands clearly visible from the mainland, now inhabited only by seals, sea lions, and birds.

Tidepools exposed near the tip of the peninsula have an extraordinary abundance of marine life. Sea stars, hermit crabs, chitons, anemonies, sea urchins and many other intertidal life forms are common; and at low tide you may see what appears to be spherical boulders several feet in diameter fastened to these tidepool rocks. Closer inspection will reveal that these objects, covered with countless tiny holes, are actually tube masses, created by calciferous tube worms. Nourished largely by sea lion and seal wastes, the waters of Año Nuevo have some of the world's largest tube worm formations. Each calcium carbonate tube mass is a community of worms and a vast network of tubal tunnels.

Harbor seals are often seen lounging on the rocks offshore, and are seen bobbing their heads above water near the shore to examine humans. Their short, plump, spotted bodies are easily identified. They mate on the island in April and May.

Humans have been visiting this area for thousands of years, as evidenced by shell mounds left by a once large Ohlone Indian habitation. For many centuries Indians lived a relatively easy life, thriving on the coast's abundance of seafood, game, acorns, and other wild edibles, and had no need for agriculture. Their discarded seashells form numerous shell mounds on this peninsula. The Indians lived in lodges usually made of willow branches arranged in 6-foot circles, bent and tied at the top, and thatched and sealed with mud.

Año Nuevo has one of the oldest place names in the country, named "La Punta De Año Nuevo" (The Point Of The New Year) by the Spanish explorer Sebastian Vizcaino on January 3, 1603. Año Nuevo Bay was used for shipping redwood timber from the Santa Cruz Mountains between 1853 and 1920, and the peninsula and vicinity was part of a cattle ranch established by Isaac Steele. The old ranger residence at the parking lot was built in 1870 for Isaac's daughter, Flora Dickerman Steele. Just north are other restored ranch buildings which now house a visitors' center and bookstore.

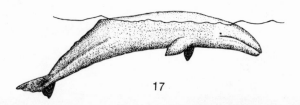

Big Basin Redwoods State Park

TO GET THERE... take **Highway 9 and turn west on Highway 236. The southern access is from Boulder Creek.**

Big Basin is a large and diverse land of dark redwood groves, sunny ridges, and rocky peaks. This is the largest park in the Santa Cruz Mountains, with enough miles of trails to satisfy the most enthusiastic of hikers. Here you will find more than 35 miles of trails, which allow hikers to escape the crowded paved areas and explore some of the mountains' most beautiful semi-wilderness.

The wildest and most spectacular hike in Big Basin is the 10 mile Berry Creek-Sunset trail loop. Take an entire day and enjoy the waterfalls and remote first-growth redwood groves, stopping often to appreciate the wonderful variety of scenery. This is not an easy hike, and it has plenty of ups and downs to encourage you to slow down and enjoy your rambles. The trail has a million rewards any time of year, but most people like it best in the late winter and early spring when everything is fresh and green and Berry Creek and Silver falls are awesome torrents, plunging more than 50 feet over mossy and fern-adorned sandstone cliffs. Upstream is Golden Falls, named for the coloring of its 20 foot sandstone escarpment.

The 'Berry Creek and Sunset trails wander far from the park's crowded paved areas and pass through all the region's ecological communities. To find this route, take the Redwood Trail past the campfire circle to Opal Creek Trail, which connects with the Berry Creek and Sunset trails. Allow at least 6 hours of hiking to cover this trail. You can make a 2 day hike out of this route by camping at Sunset Trail-

Berry Creek Falls is a raging torrent after winter rains.

camp a short distance across Berry Creek on the Sunset Trail. It is about 5.5 miles from park headquarters.

The Howard King Trail can be taken as a longer and more strenuous alternative to the Berry Creek Falls Trails. Take the Hihn Hammond dirt road up 1,840 foot high McAbee Mountain and turn right on the trail. This route has some great views, especially of the Waddell Creek canyon to the southwest.

The trail to Pine Mountain and Buzzards Roost is a strenuous but scenic 5 mile round trip climb of more than 1,000 feet from park headquarters. The climb to the 2,208 foot summit of Pine Mountain is a journey above the redwoods to an ecological island of madrone, knobcone pine, and chapparal. The weathered sandstone summit of Buzzards Roost offers the best views of the two peaks. To take this hike, follow the Opal Creek Trail south and turn right on Pine Mountain Trail. Be sure to bring water, as there is none available on the peaks.

The knobcone pine is well suited for these dry and rocky ridgetops. It is found mostly in dry areas with poor soil, where most other trees do poorly. This hardy pine needs the direct sunlight of hilltops and ridges and is dependent on fire to remove competing vegetation and for generating sufficient heat to release seeds from the cones. Put one of the cones in your oven and watch it open up and expel its seeds as the heat rises. You will also see knobcone pines on the Sunset Trail.

There is a strenuous one-day hike, or a moderate two-day backpacking trip on a scenic and diverse 14-mile loop trail through the park's northern mountains. From park headquarters walk the Opal Creek Trail upstream (north) and take the "Skyline-to-the-Sea" trail east to China Grade Road or Rim Trail, which climbs north and west to the new Lane Sunset trailcamp, built with a grant from Lane Publishing. This is a spectacular place to spend a night, with a remote wilderness feel to it. Call park headquarters for reservations. To complete the loop follow the ridge westward to the Johansen Road and the Middle Ridge Trail, which is actually a dirt road. It follows a scenic ridge southbound, past Ocean View Summit. Take Sunset Trail east to the Opal Creek Trail and back to park headquarters. This hike passes through all the park's ecological zones and involves a climb of more than 1,300 feet. Don't forget to bring drinking water, especially in summer.

If that one is too tough, you might want to go to the other extreme and take the easiest trail in the park. Just west of the parking lot near park headquarters is Redwood Trail, an easy self-guiding nature loop by some of the largest trees in the park. The trail is less than a mile long and makes an easy family stroll.

Big Basin Redwoods State Park has facilities for trail and car camping, fishing, a grocery store, and a nature museum. For more information and camping reservations, call park headquarters at (408) 338-6132.

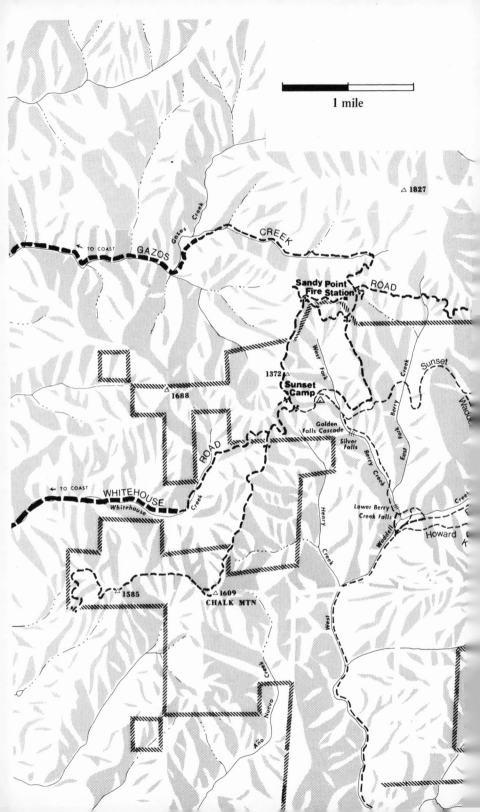

1 mile

△ 1827

TO COAST
GAZOS CREEK CREEK ROAD
Gazos Creek

Sandy Point
Fire Station

West Fork
1372 △
Sunset Camp
Sunset
Berry Creek
Waddell

△ 1688
ROAD

Golden Falls Cascade
Silver Falls
East Fork Berry Creek

TO COAST
WHITEHOUSE
Whitehouse Creek

Henry Creek
Berry Creek
Lower Berry Creek Falls
Waddell
Howard
Creek

△ 1585
△ 1609
CHALK MTN

Nuevo Creek
Año

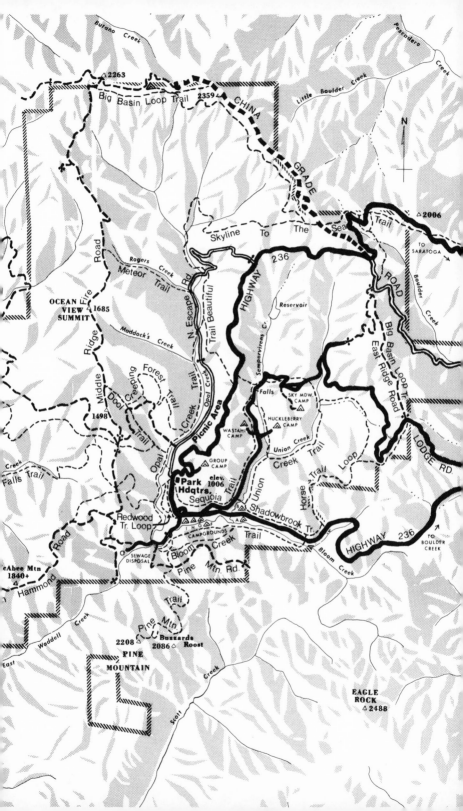

Rancho Del Oso

With the addition of the 1,700 acre "Rancho Del Oso,"Big Basin now extends all the way to Highway 1 on the coast. The popular "Skyline-to-the-Sea" trail has been re-routed through this beautiful and historic property along Waddell Creek. The distance from park headquarters to the coast is about 11 miles of easy and scenic hiking through the steep and forested Waddell Canyon which becomes broad and grassy on the coast.

There are 3 trailcamps in "Rancho Del Oso": Camp Herbert is about 7.5 miles from Big Basin park headquarters; Twin Redwoods is 1.5 miles downstream from Camp Herbert; and Alder Camp is less than a mile downstream from Twin Redwoods. Highway 1 is 1.2 miles downstream from Alder Camp. Ground fires are prohibited here and campers are encouraged to make reservations by calling park headquarters. For a detailed topographic map of this area send a self-addressed, stamped envelope and 35 cents to Sempervirens Fund, P.O. Box 1141 Los Altos, California 94022.

"Rancho Del Oso" may be reached from Highway 1 about 15 miles north of Santa Cruz, where Waddell Creek meets the coast; or from Big Basin park headquarters by way of the Berry Creek Falls or Howard King trails.

This canyon was explored by Captain Gaspar de Portola in October 1769 when his scurvey-plagued expedition paused for three days of recuperation. Because of their rapid recovery the crew dubbed the canyon "Canada de la Salud" (Canyon of Health). William Waddell came to the canyon in 1862 and built a lumber mill at the confluence of the East and West forks of Waddell Creek, which was connected by a five mile tramway to a wharf at Ano Nuevo Bay. He was killed by an irate grizzly bear here in 1875. Theodore J. Hoover, brother of President Herbert Hoover, bought the property in 1913 and it was held by the family until purchased by the state.

Redwood and Douglas fir thrive in the valleys and shady north-facing slopes, and especially on the moist seaward side of the range. A walk through the redwoods is a journey to the prehistoric past. These stately giants are a remnant of an ancient race dating back 100 million years, and the dozen or more kinds of ferns found here are descendents of some of the earliest members of the plant kingdom.

San Jose photographer Andrew P. Hill (1853-1922) was the main force behind the establishment of the park in 1901. Hill was photographing redwoods for a British publication in 1899 when the owner of the redwood grove accused him of trespassing and demanded his negatives. Hill angrily refused and returned to San Jose to start a crusade to save the redwoods. He wrote that "the thought flashed through my mind that these trees, because of their size and antiquity, were among the natural wonders of the world and should be saved for posterity."

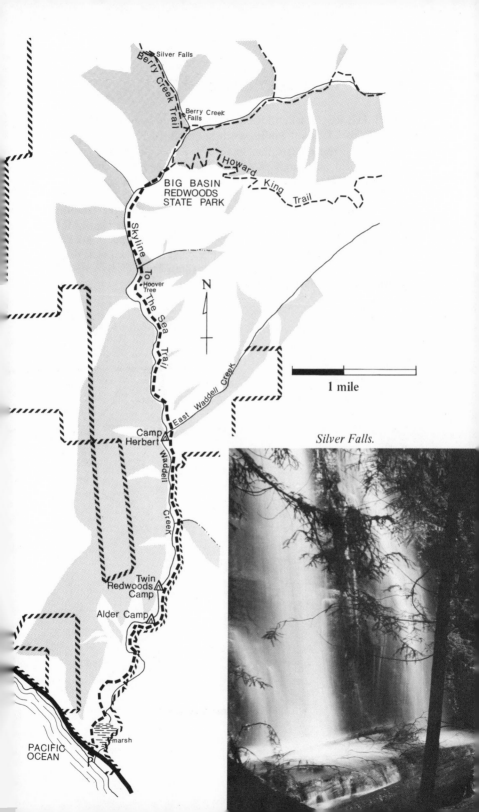

Silver Falls.

Butano State Park

TO GET THERE . . . take Cloverdale Road about 3 miles east of Highway 1. The park is about 5 miles south of Pescadero.

It is hard to overstate the charm of this cool, green canyon park. It has a magical rain forest garden of redwoods and ferns cupped between steep ridges, which can be climbed for sweeping vistas.

The easiest hike in the park is on the Creek Trail which can be started on the left side of the road just before reaching the campfire center. This trail is short and mostly level and follows the heavily forested creek bed. More strenuous paths take hikers to the Olmo Fire Trail on the south ridge and the Butano Fire Trail on the north ridge. The Ano Nuevo Trail, stemming from the Olmo Trail, offers a view of Ano Nuevo Island and the ocean on clear days.

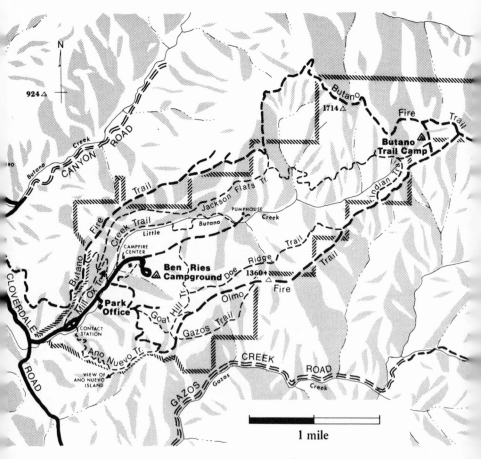

Serious backpackers should consider hiking the ridgetop loop trail to Butano Trailcamp, which can be reached by following the Doe Ridge Trail up a gradual grade to the Olmo Fire Road. Then turn left on the Indian Trail and head about 200 yards to the Fire Road near the trailcamp. The Butano Fire Trail continues to the Jackson Flats Trail which returns to the park entrance area. This hike is about 5.5 miles each way and involves some vigorous hill climbing and a gain of about 1,400 feet to the trailcamp. Enthusiastic hikers may want to make a day of it and hike the loop in one day. Be sure to make reservations in advance to use the camp from May to October by calling park headquarters.

A few miles can be lopped off the loop by continuing on the Indian Trail into the canyon and on to the Jackson Flats Trail.

Hikers with truly extraordinary enthusiasm may want to consider continuing on the Olmo Fire Trail all the way to Big Basin. The legality of hiking this route is still in doubt and camping is not permitted along the way.

Butano State Park is a 2,200 acre enclave of redwoods in the coastal fog belt on the west side of the range. One of its joys is the absence of crowds. Because of its out of the way location you can often walk for hours without passing another hiker.

The Indians usually avoided the shady groves for both practical and religious reasons. They felt the same life force that many hikers still experience today, and were convinced that redwoods were haunted by powerful spirits. That wasn't the only reason they had to stay away, though. The main reason was that edible plants, for both man and deer, are rare in the redwood groves, and the Indians found happier hunting grounds elsewhere. You will notice, however, that redwood forest creekbeds usually have no shortage of banana slugs, salamanders, and newts, and that in addition to steller jays you are likely to see Pygmy nuthatches, chestnut-backed chikadees, winter wrens, and golden-crowned kinglets flying overhead.

In addition to the trailcamp there is also a walk-in campground for car campers. For camping reservations and information call park headquarters at (415) 879-0173.

Calero Reservoir County Park

TO GET THERE . . . from Highway 101 take Bailey Ave. southwest to McKean Road. Turn right for reservoir access; turn left for trail access and park at the entrance to Calero Farm.

This is one of the noisiest and quietest places in the Santa Cruz Mountains. The reservoir itself is noisy with urban refugees on summer weekends when the lake water is warm and inviting. Powerboats roar with pleasure, and this may seem the last place to find a little solitude.

A quick study of the map, however, reveals that most of this 2,284-acre park lies south of the reservoir and that a large area is now being enjoyed almost exclusively by equestrians and cows.

From Bailey, drive south on McKean a little under a mile to the entrance to Calero Farm. At the road that goes to the farm you will notice a wooden gate at the dirt road trail that loops through the park. Turn right on the first intersecting dirt road which passes a small pond and swings down to near the farm and then up and over the ridge. This route intersects the dirt road you started on and takes you back. The total distance is about 4 miles of easy walking. These generous grassy hills are kept trimmed by the persistent effort of grazing cattle, and are studded with park-like displays of oak, bay, and elderberry. None of the trails are marked, though, so keep your bearings.

On the dry southeast part of the Santa Cruz range, Calero has a pronounced split personality. From lush and green during the rainy season, to crisp and brown in the dry months, this park is worth visiting all through the year.

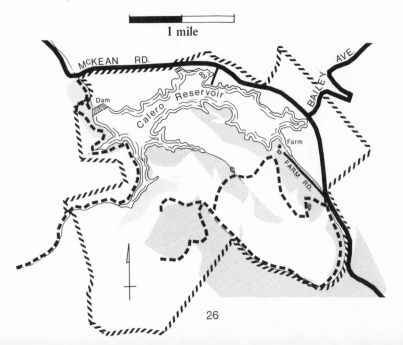

1 mile

Castle Rock State Park

TO GET THERE... take Skyline Boulevard about 3 miles south from its intersection with Highway 9 (Saratoga Gap).

Spectacular views in all directions, rock outcroppings ideal for climbing, waterfalls, and beautiful groves of oak, madrone, and Douglas fir make this one of my favorite parks.

Castle Rock itself is one of the Bay Area's most popular climbing rocks because of its challenging overhangs and impressive posture on the crest of the range. You can see the ocean and San Francisco Bay from the top. This 80-foot sandstone outcropping, however, is sometimes so congested that climbers must wait their turn to rappel off the summit.

This park covers 2,700 acres and has more than 14 miles of excellent trails. Hiking, picnicking, rock climbing, and backpacking are favorite activities here. To reach some of the outlying areas take the Ridge Trail heading uphill (north) from Castle Rock Trail east of the waterfall. Goat Rock, with its formidable south face for climbers, is easily ascended on the uphill side by hikers who marvel at the extraordinary views of Monterey Bay, the Monterey Peninsula, and the Santa Lucia Mountains 80 miles to the south. Continue west on the Ridge Trail for more views and lesser known rocks, and on to Castle Rock Trailcamp.

Climbing on Castle Rock.

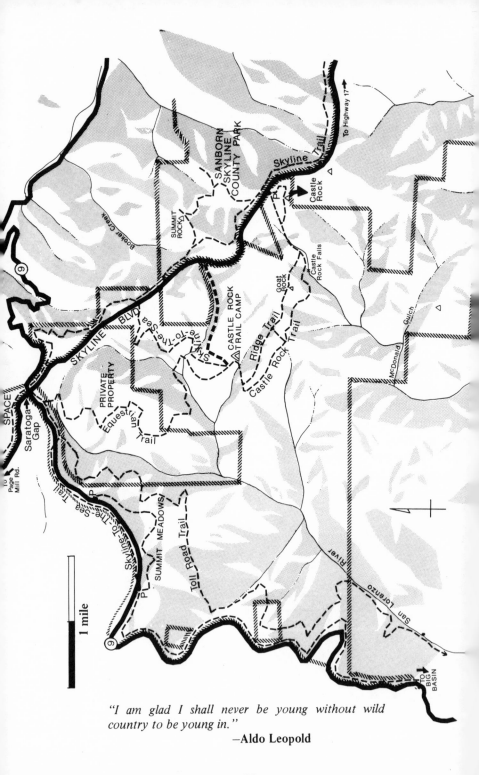

"I am glad I shall never be young without wild country to be young in."

—Aldo Leopold

Castle Rock is less than   half a mile south of the parking lot. The park's main trail, Castle Rock Trail, begins at the opposite end of the parking lot from Skyline Boulevard and continues through most of the park and on to Big Basin State Park 23.6 miles down the trail. About a mile from the parking lot on this trail is 100 foot Castle Rock Falls, an awesome sight after a heavy rain, but not much more than a trickle during the dry months.

A hike to Castle Rock Trail Camp, about 3.2 miles from the parking lot, is a moderate one day hike with plenty of beautiful views of the San Lorenzo River basin and ridges to the west. The trail is on the west slope of the skyline ridge, and offers a wonderful chance to view the effects of topography on mountain ecology. Compare the deep green of the moist evergreen valleys with the vegetation around you: oak, bay, tanoak, and madrone, as well as chaparral plants such as toyon and chamise are the plants of the dry ridgetops. Some of the most beautiful madrone and oak groves in the mountains are right here.

From the trailcamp the new re-routed "Skyline-to-the-Sea" Trail winds its way north to Saratoga Gap. The western part of this park was acquired through the efforts of the Sempervirens Fund, P.O. Box 1141, Los Altos, California 94022. At the headwaters of the San Lorenzo River, this area is steep and varied, with some of the most striking views in the range.

With its grassy promontories and Douglas fir, madrone, bay, maple, and oak woods, the newly-acquired Summit Meadows property may be explored by trail from Highway 9 west from Skyline. Threatened with development, this easily accessible parkland is an important addition to the corridor of parkland between Skyline Boulevard and Big Basin.

Chaparral is hard to love, especially for people who try to walk through it. It seems to lack much of the obvious beauty of forests and grasslands; and it's a true nightmare for cross-country hiking. It has stiff, spiny, and unyielding branches that can only be truly appreciated from wide and well worn trails. When cross-country hiking and some of this impenetrable stuff stands in your way look for deer trails that may wind through to the other side.

Though large mammals usually avoid chaparral, it is a feeding ground for many species of birds, including wrentits, scrub jays, California thrashers, goldfinches, and California quails. One of the mammals you may see here is the dusky-footed woodrat, an industrious little rodent which builds its home of sticks and twigs that may reach several feet in height.

The park's trailcamp has 25 sites, available on a first-come, first-served basis. A ranger told me that it has never been filled to capacity. For more information, call park headquarters at (408) 338-6132.

Duveneck Windmill Pasture Area

TO GET THERE. . . take Moody Road west past Foothill College in Los Altos Hills, and turn left on Rhus Ridge Road. Park at the gate near a tennis court.

Rising through the foothills of the Santa Cruz Mountains and up the steep Monte Bello Ridge, this 761-acre park has close urban proximity for casual day walks and access to adjoining parks for more strenuous outings.

From the gate, hike the short but steep dirt road to the top of the ridge. This stretch of trail is strenuous, but the rewards are great and the grade levels out when you reach the ridgetop, with wonderful panoramas of the hills and mountains to the west, including Black Mountain. At the top of the ridge the trail forks in 3 directions. Take the middle route, which heads west through the oak-studded grasslands and then swings south for a view of an old metal windmill in a grassy clearing.

A vigorous and spectacular 3.5 mile trail to the top of Black Mountain, in Monte Bello Open Space, makes an exciting and invigorating event. The trail goes through private property part of the way, so call Hidden Villa Ranch for permission: (415) 948-4690. By arranging a car shuttle you can walk about 7 scenic and inspiring miles from Windmill Pasture, up Black Mountain, and north on Monte Bello Ridge to Page Mill Road. A trailcamp near Black Mountain allows the trip to be broken into two days and allows the rare opportunity to spend a night in the grasslands east of Skyline.

The Windmill Pasture was part of the 2,300-acre Hidden Villa Ranch, which was owned by Frank and Josephine Duveneck between 1923 and 1977, when they gave it to the public as a preserve. The windmill is a remnant of the generations of ranching in these hills. Just west of the preserve is Hidden Villa Ranch, famous for its Youth Hostel and environmental education programs.

Though it is not geographically connected, this park is classified as part of the Rancho San Antonio Open Space Preserve. For further information, call the Midpeninsula Regional Open Space district at (415) 965-4717.

If you get a chance to observe scrub jays in action you might notice that they are Nature's tree planters. Scrub jays are busy little fellows who often bury acorns in the ground, and then get sidetracked by other important duties and forget where the treasure was left. They win whether they remember or not, though , since they can either eat the acorns or let them grow into oak trees for the benefit of future generations of scrub jays.

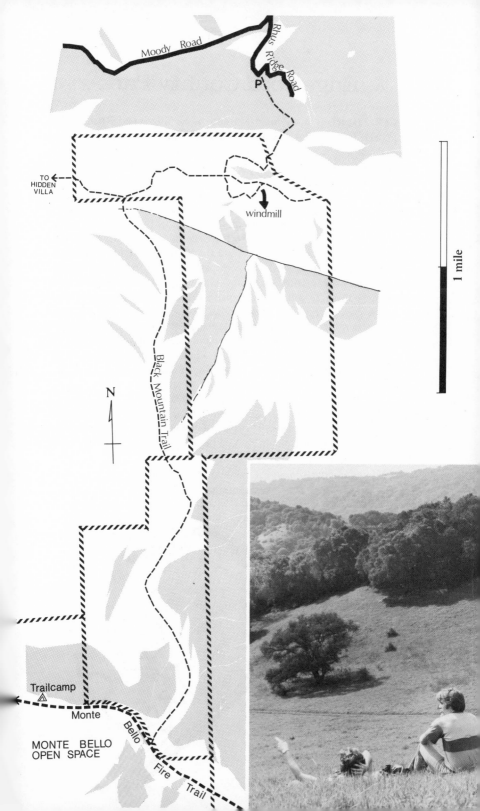

Moody Road

Rhus Ridge Road

P

TO
HIDDEN
VILLA

windmill

1 mile

N

Black Mountain Trail

Trailcamp

Monte
Bello

MONTE BELLO
OPEN SPACE

Fire Trail

Edgewood County Park

TO GET THERE . . . the main entrance is on Edgewood Road at Old Stagecoach Road opposite Crestview Drive. Other accesses are at Edgewood Road just west of Highway 280 where a trail goes under the freeway and into the park; and at the intersection of Hillcrest Way and Sunset in Redwood City.

This is a small and inviting area of rounded, grassy hills, chaparral, and oakwoods. Because of its easy access to Redwood City and vicinity, it's a wonderful place for picnics and short walks that take only a few hours out of the day, and still allow time for enjoying the views of Redwood City and the bay to the east, and the Skyline ridge to the west.

As of this writing, the 467-acre park has no formal trail system, though a network of dirt roads and clandestine paths make the area walkable. A 150-acre golf course is planned for the flatlands near 280.

The park's serpentine grasslands support "rare" and "endangered" plants. Serpentine, associated with fault zones, provides poor soil for most plants because of its high toxicity and low water-holding capacity; but encourages the growth of specially adapted vegetation. This is the only known habitat for the San Mateo Thornmint, officially designated an endangered species by the state of California.

The worst thing about this park is that some of the hillsides have been severely eroded by offroad vehicles, which tear up the vegetation that holds the soil in place. This park is being restored, however, and has real potential. I expect there will be a lot more to say about it in the next edition of this book.

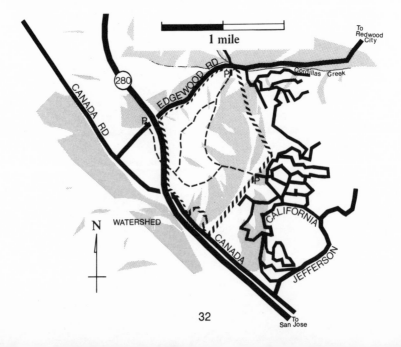

El Sereno Open Space

TO GET THERE... from Highway 17 take Montevina Road to its end where a small turnout provides parking for several cars.

This 955 acre park spans 2 miles of scenic ridgetop and steep canyons on the east side of the range. Chaparral covers most of the area, with oak, madrone, and bay scattered through the area and providing islands of shade for summer hikers; and beautiful groves of madrone and bay grow on the north and east sides of the ridge.

A good time to visit is in early spring, when chamise, ceanothus and other chaparral vegetation burst forth with new growth and are

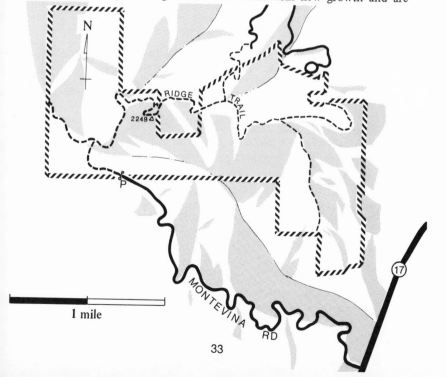

adorned with an abundance of flowers. Use your nose often here to appreciate the spicy aromas that offer a special appeal in this kind of plant community. You will see and hear lots of birds as they feed off the many seeds and berries that grow here.

Another advantage of chaparral is that it is low enough that it doesn't obstruct the commanding vistas of the Santa Cruz Mountains and the urbanized Santa Clara Valley. To the north you will see Black Mountain, Oakland, and even Mount Tamalpais, and to the southeast stands Mount Umunhum. The views are particularly stunning on those cold, crystal clear days of winter when the smog and haze are gone from the valley below.

Most of the trails through this park are dirt roads, and if you have ever tried cross-country hiking through chaparral you will appreciate why this is a good place for sticking to the established trails. Hikers should also be aware that this is one of the region's driest parks and water should be carried. Animals you might see here include woodrats, black-tail deer, rabbits, and coyotes.

This park is open for day use only. For more information, call the Midpeninsula Regional Open Space District at (415) 965-4717.

Foothills Park

TO GET THERE. . . take Page Mill Road in Palo Alto west of Highway 280.

The city of Palo Alto operates a 1,400 acre "nature preserve" in the low foothills west of town. The park, on the steep eastern slopes of the Santa Cruz Mountains, is characterized by grasslands, chaparral, oak, madrone, bay, buckeye, and a big lawn and picnic area. You may also appreciate the small reservoir for fishing near the park entrance and the nature interpretive center, near the lawn, that has an educational exhibit of native plants and animals.

These wide, grassy expanses are inhabited by multitudes of ground squirrels and the birds of prey which feed on them. Many species of birds are easily seen here – so bring binoculars.

The park changes from season to season and is pleasant for hiking all year, though my favorite time is the green, flowering months of early spring. The preserve has about 15 miles of hiking trails, including several scenic loops of 5 to 7 miles, with some nice vistas of the south Bay Area.

Unfortunately for most Bay Area hikers this park is open only to Palo Alto residents and their guests, and you will be asked for identification at the gate. For information about the regularly scheduled nature walks, call park headquarters at (415) 329-2423.

The park is open for day use only.

The Forest of Nisene Marks State Park

TO GET THERE... take the Aptos Creek Road north from Soquel Drive in Aptos.

The Forest of Nisene Marks is a vast and rugged semi-wilderness, with few of the facilities we normally expect from state parks. It's a diverse land of redwood forests, riperian woodlands, oak groves, stands of knobcone pine, and chaparral; and it has a robust pioneer history whose remnants are rotting away and becoming part of the landscape.

This park has few camping and picnicking facilities, but it has lots of hiking trails and some beautiful forest scenery. Some of these trails, however, being poorly marked, may be hard to follow and should be taken cautiously to avoid getting lost in this dense coastal redwood forest. Camping is permitted only at the trailcamp near the Sand Point Overlook, a 6 mile hike from the Aptos Creek Road trailhead by way of West Ridge Trail. It can also be reached by hiking 5.4 miles on Buzzard Lagoon Road and the Aptos Fire road past the locked gate off Eureka Canyon Road.

This forest was a source of Bay Area Lumber between 1870 and 1925 and few first-growth redwoods now remain; but some of the remnants of the lumber industry can still be found on the Loma Prieta Grade Trail, which follows an old railroad bed. Three miles from the trailhead is Hoffman's Historic Site (formerly China Camp), consisting of a few deteriorating wooden buildings and bridges dating back to the lumber boom years.

The Loma Prieta Grade and West Ridge trails wind through some steep terrain and can be strenuous for beginners; but the entire loop is only about 7 miles and at an easy pace almost anyone should be able to make it. You can hike north on the West Ridge Trail to the trailcamp. Watch out for poison oak in this area.

A strenuous loop hike of more than 19 miles, and a gain of more than 1,000 feet, can be achieved by combining the Aptos Creek Fire Road with West Ridge Trail and Loma Prieta Grade. Despite the long uphill grade, the Aptos Creek Fire Road will reward you with views of the surrounding mountains and occasionally the ocean. Fossil seashells are common in the exposed road cuts as this route climbs above the redwoods and into oak, madrone, and chaparral.

Except for the strident call of steller jays, there is often a profound sense of quiet that contributes to the cathedral qualities of the redwood groves. The tall trees let little light reach the ground, and their thick, soft bark seems to actually absorb sound and light, creating a mood of sober tranquility. I know of no other trees which can have such a profound and immediate influence on a hiker's mood. It takes only a few of the trees in a grove to create a feeling of dark dignity and quiet.

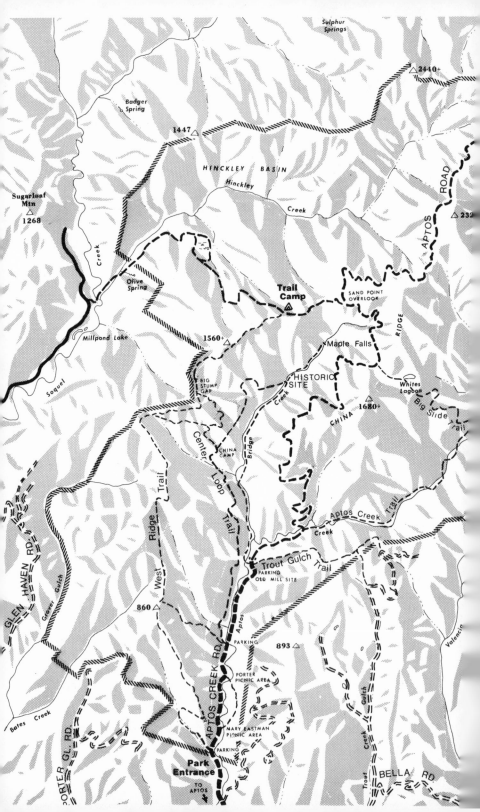

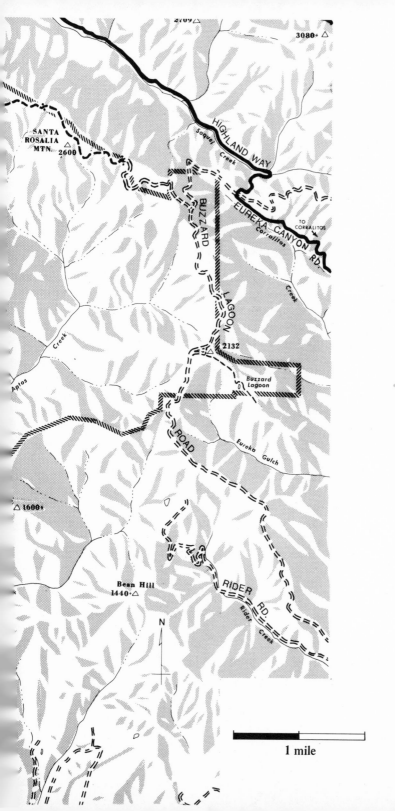

2769 △

3080+ △

HIGHLAND WAY

Soquel Creek

SANTA
ROSALIA
MTN.
2600 △

BUZZARD

EUREKA-CANYON RD.

TO
CORRALITOS

Corralitos

Creek

LAGOON

Creek

2132 △

Buzzard
Lagoon

Aptos

Creek

Eureka Gulch

ROAD

△ 1600+

Bean Hill
1440+ △

RIDER RD.

Rider Creek

N

1 mile

The park covers nearly 10,000 acres and all the creeks that flow through it originate within its boundaries. These brawling arteries of life support their own plant communities and have vertical gardens of five finger ferns hanging from their moist, shady banks.

Mountain Lions sometimes sneak through the park, though they are rarely seen. Look for their paw prints beside mud puddles after rains or along creek beds.

The park is open daily from 6 a.m. until sunset. Horses and firearms are not allowed, and ground fires are prohibited at the trailcamp. There are 2 picnic areas, both along Aptos Creek Road.

For further information and trailcamp reservations, call (408) 335-4598 or write: Henry Cowell Redwoods State Park, P.O. Box P-1, Felton, California 95018.

Materialism is a value that hiking and backpacking discourage. In civilization, the more a person has the better off he is considered to be; but in the woods the opposite is true. Hikers encumbered with a lot of possessions are at a disadvantage. You will learn quickly which property is really important when you have to carry it on your back.

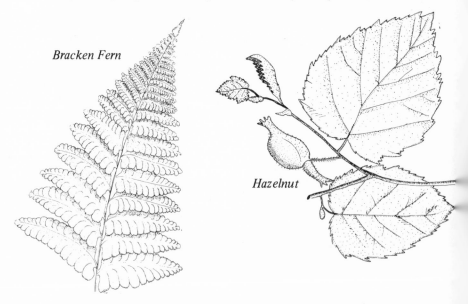

Bracken Fern

Hazelnut

"I find that the three truly great times for thinking thoughts are when I am standing in the shower, sitting on the john, or walking. And the greatest of these, by far, is walking."
— **Colin Fletcher**

Fremont Older Open Space

TO GET THERE... from Saratoga-Sunnyvale Road, take Prospect Road west to the end of the road. A trail into the park can also be taken from the Villa Maria area of Stevens Creek County Park off Stevens Canyon Road.

This 734-acre preserve near Cupertino is a low and easy land of gentle hills and leisurely walks. The 4.5 miles of trails ramble through oakwoods, grasslands, chaparral, hayfields, and remnant walnut and apricot groves that still bear fruit. Since 1870 this land has produced grapes, apricots, prunes, walnuts, and olives.

This park is a gentle blend of natural and agricultural qualities; but it still hosts a wonderful abundance of wildlife. Deer roam freely, squirrels trapeze across the green leafy forest canopy, and woodpeckers tap holes in oak trees. I also discovered that rattlesnakes make their home here. Bounding down a steep hill I heard a rattling sound that let me know that I was getting too close to a disgruntled snake. I leaped to a respectable distance from the startled serpent and watched him glide into the bushes. Despite a bad reputation, they are actually good natured fellows who usually try to avoid trouble — and they even sound a warning when people get too close.

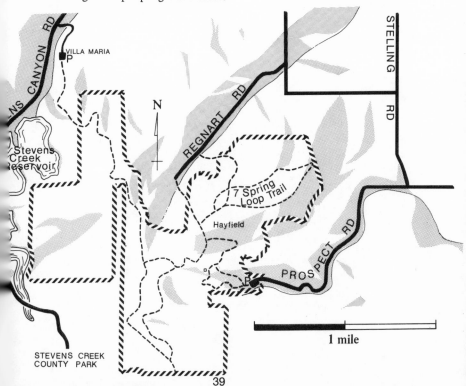

The home of distinguished San Francisco newspaper editor Fremont Older, which was originally built in 1911, has been faithfully restored and is open to the public occasionally for group tours. The property was purchased by the Midpeninsula Regional Open Space District in 1975, and the house is under private lease.

The park is open from dawn to dusk and fire arms and motor vehicles are prohibited. Be sure to carry water, especially during the summer months. Most of the park's trails are dirt ranch roads. For more information, call the Midpeninsula Regional Open Space District at (415) 965-4717.

The Open Space District

The Midpeninsula Regional Open Space District is an independent special district established by the voters to protect places of scenic and ecological value within easy access to the cities of northern Santa Clara and southern San Mateo counties.

The preserves are open for quiet activities such as walking, picnicking, nature study, and horseback riding. They also protect valuable wildlife habitat, and help to hold the line against urban sprawl.

Nature walks and other organized activities are conducted by volunteer docents trained by the district with the cooperation of Foothill College. If you want to be a docent, or go on a docent walk, call (415) 965-4717 for details.

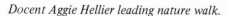

Docent Aggie Hellier leading nature walk.

Henry Cowell Redwoods State Park

TO GET THERE. . . The southern unit is just south of Felton on Highway 9. The Fall Creek unit is just northwest of town on the Felton-Empire Road.

This redwood-forested park is divided into 2 sizable units in the mountains near Felton.

Most visitors are unaware that the popular Redwood Grove and picnic area just south of Felton are only a small part of the park. The great bulk of the southern unit of this redwood preserve can be reached by well developed hiking trails from several roadside pullouts on Highway 9, from the park campground on Graham Hill Road, and from the picnic area near park headquarters (the day use entrance). This unit covers 1,737 acres and has about 15 miles of hiking trails.

The Redwood Grove nature trail loop (near the picnic area) is the easiest and most popular trail in the park. It is less than 1 mile and

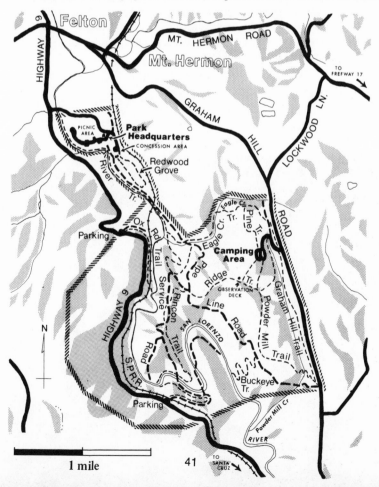

1 mile

is more of a stroll than a real hike, though it winds through one of the finest first-growth redwood groves south of San Francisco, and is especially pleasant on weekdays when the crowds are gone. Most of the redwoods in the rest of the park are second-growth.

This is a hilly park, and the vegetation corresponds to the area's geography. Lower areas are forested with redwood and riperian vegetation in places, and ridges and hilltops are covered with oak, madrone, digger pine, manzanita, and other chaparral plants. The distribution of plants is also connected to the availability of sunlight. Chaparral plants prefer the sunny ridgetops, while the understory plants of the redwood groves are satisfied with only indirect light and with occasional shafts of sunlight that penetrate the dense forest canopy.

A cross section of the park's ecology can be viewed on a short hike from the picnic area to the observation deck on the Ridge Trail, which climbs from the redwood-covered streambeds to the chaparral-covered ridgetops where a view of Santa Cruz and Monterey Bay are possible on clear days. The route is steep in places and there is little water along most of the trail, especially in summer. The trail, however, is only slightly more than 3 miles and is easily completed in 2 hours by most hikers. The observation deck, on the water tank at the highest point of the trail, is a good place to relax and eat lunch.

The Fall Creek Unit

The Fall Creek unit is a steep, forested, and completely magnificent 2,335 acre park, tucked into a rugged canyon northwest of Felton. Start from the parking lot just off Felton-Empire Road and hike upstream. Where the north and south forks of Fall Creek meet, follow the

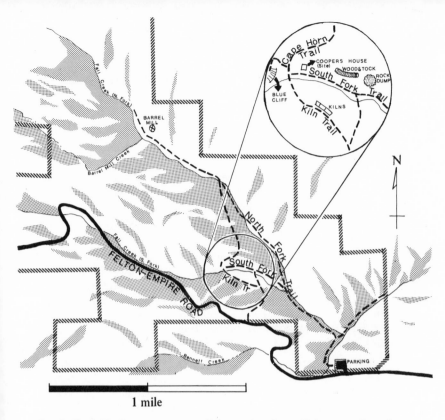

1 mile

South Fork Trail upstream to a flat area in a beautiful grove of maples, which becomes a brilliant blaze of color in autumn.

Most of this deep and shady canyon is occupied by second-growth redwoods, along with bay, big-leaf maple, and douglas fir. The forest floor is carpeted with sorrel, wild ginger, several kinds of ferns, and Solomon's seal, and chaparral grows on a few dry places.

Here the IXL Lime Company built 3 lime kilns in 1870, which were fired with split redwood logs, some of which are still stacked across the creek from the kilns. By 1880 this was one of the state's most important lime producers. Above these deteriorated kilns rises Blue Cliff, an old limestone quarry.

From the kiln area hike the Cape Horn Trail to the North Fork Trail and follow the creek upstream to the scattered remains of a water-powered barrel mill which was built in 1912. From here hike down-stream and back to the trailhead.

Fall Creek itself is one of the park's most wonderful features. It bounces wild and cold all summer, splashing over granite boulders which make it reminiscent of High Sierra streams. This beautiful canyon has more delightful qualities than I can mention here and is one of my favorite places in the Santa Cruz Mountains.

For more information, call park headquarters at (408) 335-4598.

Huddart County Park

TO GET THERE ... take Woodside Road 3.5 miles west from Highway 280 and turn north on Kings Mountain Road.

This is one of San Mateo County's most popular parks, and its many recreational facilities often make it more crowded than most hikers like. Fortunately, however, you can leave the parking lots and picnic areas behind and explore about 15 miles of trails. The park covers 973 acres of oak woodlands, chaparral, and Douglas fir and redwood forests.

This is a very steep park, with trails to match. The gentlest hiking route is along the Richard's Road Trail — Dean Trail by West Union Creek. From here, a variety of trails climb to the Skyline ridge at 2,000 feet. Easy walkers may want to take the .75 mile nature trail near the park entrance station. For a more ambitious loop hike, combine the Archery Fire Trail, the Summit Springs Trail, and the Richard's Road Trail for a complete tour of the park's unpaved parts.

This route offers a cross section of Santa Cruz Mountains ecology. Oak woodlands cover the park's lower elevations, with chaparral on dry ridgetops and redwood groves are tucked into streambed furrows. Tanoak, madrone, bay, Douglas fir, and several species of oak also contribute to this plant kingdom hodgepodge. The park's animal inhabitants include Black-tail deer, squirrels, racoons, foxes, bobcats, woodrats, several species of lizards and snakes, and an abundant variety of birds.

One of the coast redwood's most remarkable features is its ability to clone one tree into another. Redwoods produce seeds, but their primary method of reproduction is sprouting, especially around the bases of mature trees. As these sprouts grow, and the mother tree dies and decays away, a "family circle" of large trees will form with an empty space in the center.

An understanding of the human history of the park is important for an appreciation of what you will see here. The redwood groves you see are second-growth descendants of an ancient forest of giants that was logged in the 1850's and 60's to supply the Bay Area's booming cities with lumber. You can still see massive stump remnants of the original forest and trace the "skid road" depressions up the hillsides, created by oxen dragging logs to the nearby sawmills.

This park has more than the usual recreational opportunties. A childrens' playground, a horse ring, bridle paths, picnicking and barbecuing facilities, and an archery range are provided, and an overnight campground is open in summer on a first-come, first-serve basis.

For more information, call the park at (415) 851-0326.

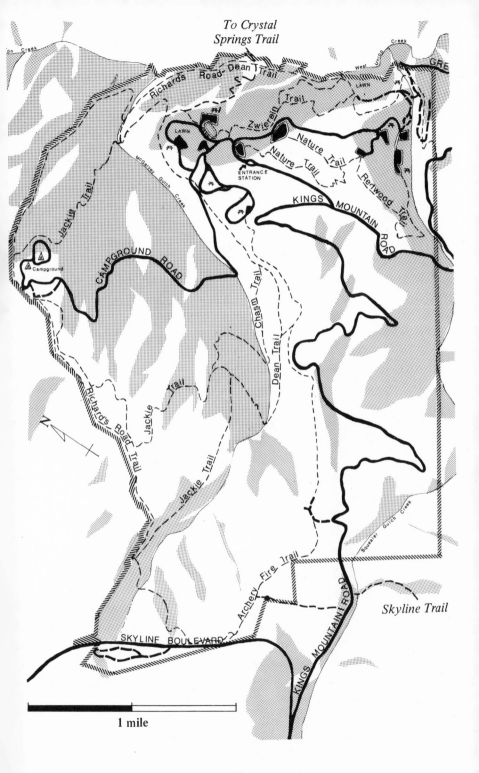

To Crystal Springs Trail

1 mile

Skyline Trail

45

HIKING FROM HUDDART: The Crystal Springs Trail.

The Crystal Springs hiking and riding trail connects Huddart Park with San Bruno Avenue in San Bruno. It goes from Huddart to Raymundo Road and resumes a fifth of a mile up the road, paralleling Highway 280 and Canada Road. The distance to San Bruno is 12 miles; to the Pulgas Water Temple is 4.2 miles. This route is popular with equestrians, though many walkers won't like the flatness and tameness of the route, or the sights and sounds of traffic on Highway 280 and Canada Road.

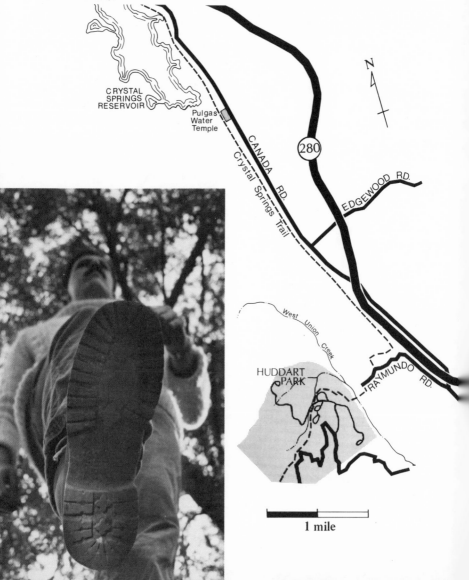

HIKING FROM HUDDART: The Skyline Trail.

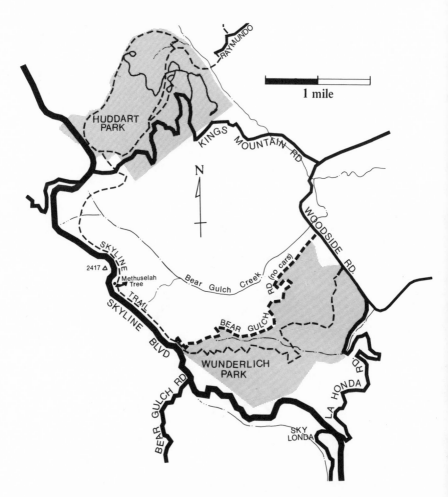

San Mateo County's ongoing Skyline Corridor Trail may be explored from Huddart Park. A scenic ridgetop riding and hiking trail follows Skyline Boulevard for about 5 miles between Huddart and Wunderlich county parks. Passing through the California Water Company's Bear Gulch Watershed, this trail passes near the "Methuselah" redwood. At 15 feet in diameter and estimated to be 1,500 years old, this is one of the few old-growth giants left in this area. A car shuttle between Huddart and Wunderlich will make this trail the key link in a grand all-day excursion.

Long Ridge Open Space

TO GET THERE . . . park at the Grizzly Flat turnout on Skyline Boulevard, 3 miles south of Page Mill Road, and 3.5 miles north of Saratoga Gap (Skyline and Highway 9). The turnout is identified by a gate and wooden fence, and is near a "Palo Alto City Limit" sign.

This place is full of adventure. It has no formal trails, and most of the routes that pass for trails are either roads or are unmarked and in terrible condition. Another problem is that some of the old ranch roads don't stay within the preserve, making it hard to avoid trespassing.

Don't be discouraged. This is a magnificent mountain park, with steep airy vistas of the ocean, and shady bay, oak, and Douglas fir groves tucked into the mountain matrix — and it's worth the trouble.

From the Grizzly Flat turnout cross Skyline, climb over or through the barbed wire fence, and head down the grassy slope to the

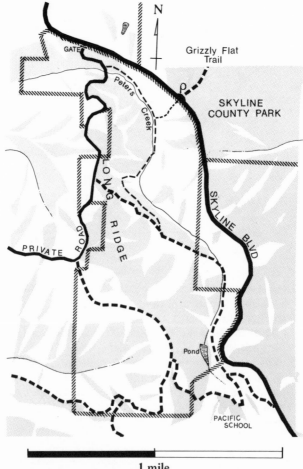

1 mile

faint remnants of the old ranch road at the bottom of the valley where the grass ends and the forest begins. Follow this elusive route as it plunges into the woodlands, crosses a creek, and climbs the ridge to where it intersects a more substantial old ranch road.

You will probably notice other paths made by deer and former human inhabitants. Give them a try; Long Ridge is for adventure.

An easier access to the area is on the private paved road just north of Grizzly Flat on Skyline. This road can be used to make a loop through the preserve.

Los Trancos Open Space

TO GET THERE... take Page Mill Road 5 miles west from Highway 280. The parking lot is uphill from Foothill Park and about 1 mile east of Skyline Boulevard.

This 274 acre park, with about 5 miles of trails, is one of my favorite nature study areas. An easy trail loops through grasslands, chaparral, and oak woods, and offers sweeping views of the bay, Mount Diablo, and San Francisco. Los Trancos straddles a revealing part of the 600 mile long San Andreas Fault, and displays many features that evidence fault activity. The trail passes Los Trancos Creek, which follows an old line of broken rock within the San Andreas fault zone. Posts with yellow bands and tops mark the location of known fault fractures.

Sag ponds, pressure ridges, and terraces in the park were created by the buckling of the rock under pressure from fault movement. Near the parking lot you will find conglomerate rocks that were sheared from Loma Prieta, a mountain 25 miles to the south, and were transported here by the gradual movement of land along the fault. The earth's crust is divided into massive plates of rock floating in the earth's mantle—and this is where 2 of them scrape together. East of here is the North American continental plate, and west is the Pacific plate. Naturalist tours leave from the parking lot on Sundays, and they are well worth attending. For more information, call the Midpeninsula Regional Open Space District at (415) 965-4717.

This is one of the Bay Area's most brilliant wildflower gardens in April when iridescent fields of blue-eyed grass, poppies, buttercups, and many others form a flowery carpet. This is also a good kite flying and picnicking spot. Madrone and bay trees are common here, as are black, blue, canyon live, and coast live oaks.

Los Trancos can be used as a starting point for exploring other open space preserves to the south, and you can even hike about 8 miles from here to Saratoga Gap, where the "Skyline-to-the-Sea" trail begins. This trans-park route can be started on Page Mill Road just downhill from the parking lot.

Docent Dave Boore demonstrates San Andreas Fault movement at Los Trancos.

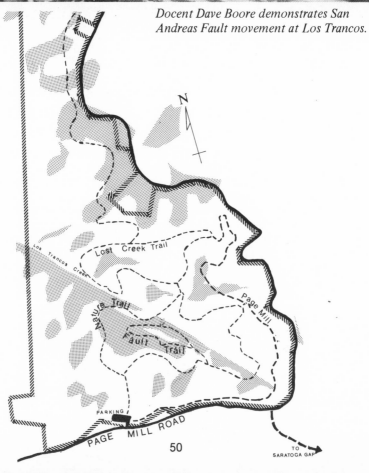

Monte Bello Open Space

TO GET THERE . . . take Page Mill Road about 5 miles west from Highway 280 to the parking area just downhill from the Los Trancos parking lot.

The largest unit of the Midpeninsula Regional Open Space District, Monte Bello is a large and varied land of deep wooded canyons, windswept grassy ridges, and the San Andreas Fault.

This park is the hub of a lot of walking opportunities. Los Trancos Open Space is just uphill and to the north; the Duveneck Windmill Pasture Area is reached by trail to the east via Black Mountain; Skyline County Park, Saratoga Gap Open Space, and Long Ridge Open Space are reached by trail to the south; and Skyline Ranch Open Space is right across Skyline Boulevard. And for the truly ambitious, it's about 8 miles from Page Mill Road to Saratoga Gap, and another 28 miles to the ocean — all on excellent and well marked trails.

From the parking area on Page Mill Road, take the Canyon Fire Trail south, pausing to appreciate gnarled old oaks and abandoned walnut orchards. Next to the trail is a marshy sag pond filled with cattails and other aquatic plants. This pond is right on a fracture of the San Andreas Fault, and was formed when the land dropped. Evidence of fault movement is common here, especially on the Geology Trail (to be built in the Spring of 1982) where the unstable ground is landsliding. A nature trail is also scheduled for construction in 1982 that will form an easy and enjoyable loop route when connected with the Canyon Fire Trail.

If you wander off the beaten paths you may come across a deteriorating old tepee, a children's swing set, and a lot of other relics from the late 1960s and early 1970s when this was a commune called "The Land."

The Indian Creek Fire Trail is one of the preserve's more vigorous walks, climbing the Monte Bello Ridge for commanding vistas of the Bay Area and the Santa Cruz Mountains. From here you can explore the Monte Bello Fire Trail, or take the Black Mountain Trail down to the Duveneck Windmill Pasture Area and Hidden Villa.

Just west of Black Mountain is the Black Mountain Ranch Trailcamp. What a place to sleep: coyote serenades, with owl counterpoint melodies; and the whole urban spectacle sprawled out below. Camping here is by permit only and open fires are prohibited. Camp stoves are allowed. For permits and information, call the open space office at (415) 965-4742.

As better parking facilities are provided on Page Mill Road, there will be more docent walks to help the public unravel the geological and ecological mysteries of this preserve. And I also hope there will eventually be better public access to the other end of the preserve at the up-hill end of Monte Bello Road, via Stevens Canyon Road, from Cupertino. This area has excellent trails and some of the most striking views in the Santa Cruz Mountains. Docent tours for 5 to 25 people can be scheduled by calling the Midpeninsula Regional Open Space District at (415) 965-4717. This 3.5-mile guided walk is jammed with scenery and history, and you may be able to stop at a winery just down the road on your way back.

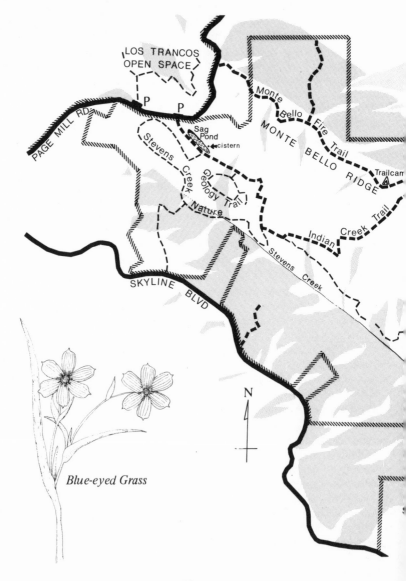

Blue-eyed Grass

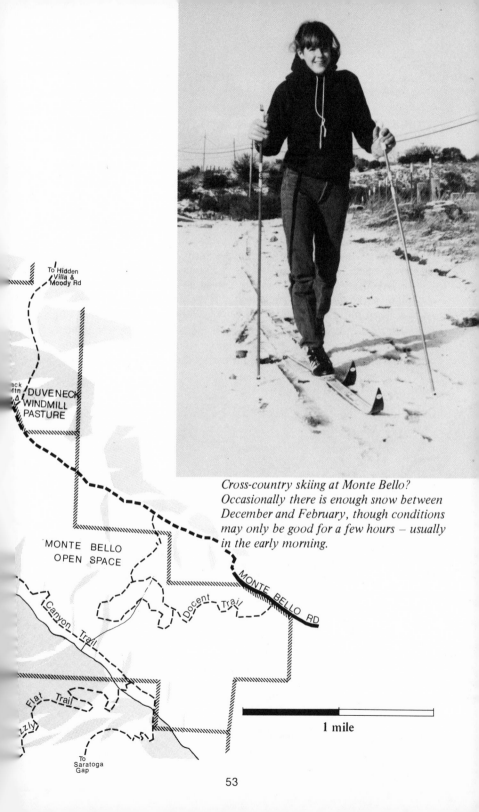

To Hidden
Villa &
Moody Rd

ack
Mtn
DUVENECK
WINDMILL
PASTURE

MONTE BELLO
OPEN SPACE

Canyon   Trail

Docent   Trail

MONTE BELLO RD

Flat   Trail

zzly

To
Saratoga
Gap

*Cross-country skiing at Monte Bello?
Occasionally there is enough snow between
December and February, though conditions
may only be good for a few hours – usually
in the early morning.*

1 mile

Mount Madonna County Park

TO GET THERE. . .take Hecker Pass Highway (Route 152) west from Gilroy.

This is a park for people who like scenic diversity, panoramic vistas, and steep trails. The park has more than 17 miles of foot and bridle trails which explore peaceful groves of redwood and oak, snake through scratchy expanses of chaparral, and gallop across open grassy hills. The park has 3,093 acres and plenty of room for even the most undauntable of hikers. To further tax your energy, it straddles a ridge-top and few of the trails come anywhere close to being level.

One of the steepest trails goes to Sprig Lake, a small but deep reservoir open to fishing by visitors between the ages of 5 and 12.

The Merry-Go-Round Trail is a steep and scenic whirlwind tour of all the park's ecological communities. It is especially pleasant in early spring when the grassy areas at the lower elevations turn green and are splashed with flowery colors. A 5 mile loop can be made by combining the Miller, Loop, Merry-Go-Round, Contour, and Ridge trails. Begin the hike just past park headquarters at the end of the road.

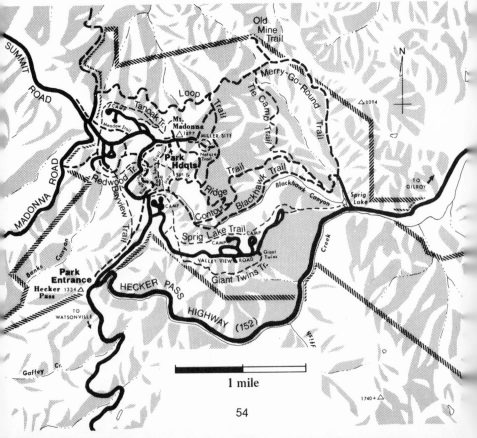

1 mile

Redwoods thrive in the coastal fog, which reduces evaporation through the critical drought months by lowering air temperatures and by lessening the exposure to direct sunlight. It makes another important contribution that most people would never guess: "fog drip". Heavy fog condenses into little water droplets on the needles of redwood trees and then drip down to other drops below, picking up momentum and dropping to the ground like a regular rainfall. This can be an important source of moisture, especially in summer, and an unfortunate hazard for unwary campers. Several summers ago I car camped under a redwood tree in this park, having failed to bring a tent because of our lack of summer rain. About 3 a.m. I awoke wet and cold and hastily ran to my car to escape what I though was a rare and rather heavy summer rain. The next morning, to my surprise, I saw that only the area immediately under the redwood tree was wet, and that I would have kept dry if I had slept just 30 feet away.

Picnicking and camping facilities are available on a first-come, first-served basis. For information, call park headquarters at (408) 842-2341.

Pescadero Creek County Park

TO GET THERE. . .it is accessible from San Mateo Memorial and Sam McDonald county parks and Portola State Park.

This is a large forested park on the watershed of one of the Santa Cruz Mountains' major creeks. For years this 6,000-acre park was used largely for reaching adjoining parks; but now there are two trail camps which make Pescadero a major target for backpackers. From Sam McDonald County Park, Tarwater Flat Trailcamp is 5 miles, and Shaw Flat Trailcamp is 4 miles. For reservations, call (415) 363-4021.

A trail connecting San Mateo County Memorial Park and Portola State Park passes through Pescadero Creek County Park. Finding the trail may be a problem, so be sure to ask directions at park headquarters if in doubt. The approximately 6 mile trail from Memorial Park can be started at the swimming area by the dam on Pescadero Creek. Follow Pescadero Creek Trail east to Wurr Road at the bridge and turn right, continuing the route south a short distance to a small wooden bridge on the left side of the road. The fire road which begins here continues through Pescadero Creek County Park.

The entrance to Portola State Park is the first fire road to the left beyond the fire road to the Sherriff's Honor Camp. The route is well maintained and easy to follow once it has been found, and can even be bicycled. The grade is relatively level, requiring little strenuous hiking, and a moderately fit hiker should be able to hike one way in about 3 hours.

Pescadero Creek County Park was heavily logged earlier in this century and today has few virgin redwoods, and evidence of logging is still visible. Rusting logging cables can still be found wrapped around redwood trunks and notches for loggers' springboards can still be found on old redwood stumps. It has been estimated that the Santa Cruz Mountains have yielded more than 10 billion feet of lumber since the Gold Rush. This land was acquired by the county to be dammed and flooded by a reservoir. When the plan was abandoned the land became a park.

A permit to enter this park may be obtained at either San Mateo County Memorial Park or at Sam McDonald County Park.

SEE MAP ON PAGE 58

Portola State Park

TO GET THERE...take Alpine Road west from Skyline Boulevard and turn south on Portola State Park Road.
Since 1945 Bay Area hikers have been exploring this redwood-forested park along Pescadero Creek. Its 1,740 acres offer more than 10 miles of trails through mostly second-growth redwood groves, though a few stands of big trees somehow survived. The park also offers opportunities for car and trail camping, fishing, and swimming.

The park's self-guided nature loop trail, which can be started just behind park headquarters, is a good place to start hiking. Though it's less than a mile long, the Sequoia Trail can be connected with the Iverson Trail for a more extensive hike. The main reason for making a point of exploring this little loop trail is to see the Shell Tree, one of the Santa Cruz Mountains' most amazing sights. The tree has an impressive 17 foot diameter—yet what is most striking about it is that it seems to be a structural impossibility. The ancient tree, estimated to be at least 2,000 years old, has been completely gutted by fire, and with only a few narrow strands of living tissue reaching the ground it is a marvel that green leaves still grow from its lofty branches.

From here you can hike the Iverson Trail along Pescadero Creek, which contains water all year and has a wading pool near the visitors center. A 6 mile public trail (actually a fire road) connects Portola State Park with San Mateo County Memorial Park. The trail goes through Pescadero Creek County Park and can be reached from the Iverson Trail where it intersects a fire road southeast of Iverson Creek. This route begins beside Iverson Cabin, built in 1860, and continues uphill to its intersection with the fire road to San Mateo Memorial and Sam McDonald parks.

The Summit and Slate Creek trails can be combined to form an enjoyable hike of about 8.5 miles. The Summit Trail can be reached from the Redwood Trail which begins across the road from the Point Group Camp Area. This route goes to Slate Creek, Page Mill Site, and to a fine stand of redwoods near the trail's end at the park boundary. Before reaching the Page Mill Site there is a trailcamp about 3 miles from the trailhead at the intersection of Slate Creek Trail and a fire road.

One of the most impressive old-growth redwood groves left in the Santa Cruz Mountains was recently added to this park. Unfortunately, though, this 350-acre parcel on Peters Creek has no trail access, and the dense underbrush makes cross-country hiking difficult. A trail is planned. Another trail being planned will connect Portola with Big Basin.

For information and reservations, call park headquarters at (415) 948-9098.

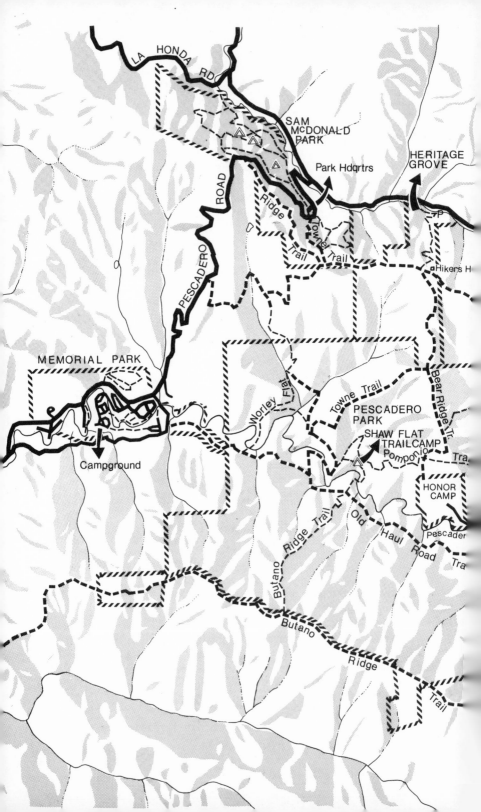

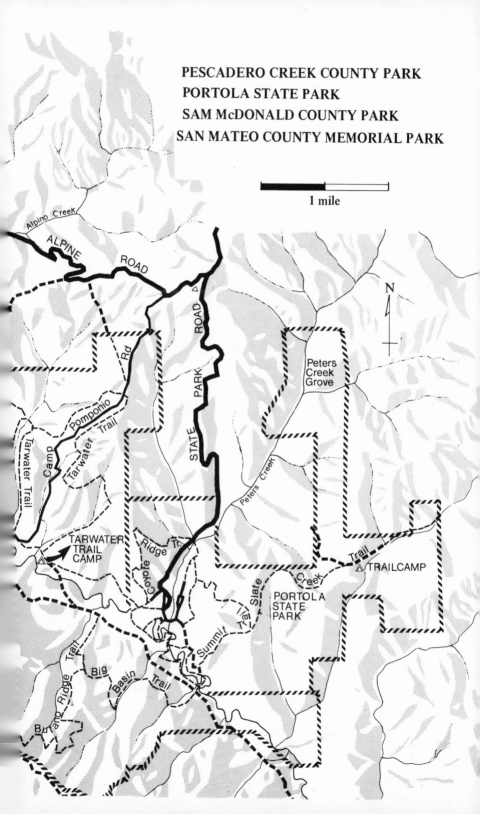

Rancho San Antonio Open Space

TO GET THERE . . . from **Highway 280 take Foothill Boulevard south
and turn west on Cristo Rey Drive. Parking is in the adjacent Rancho
San Antonio County Park.**

It is always a pleasure to find a park close enough to a city that it
can be visited by hikers who have only part of a day free. Rancho San
Antonio is such a park; and though it has only 595 acres, it is ideal for
at least half a day of exploration.

Historic Deer Hollow Farm is one of the park's most popular
features and is used for a variety of environmental education programs by the city of Mountain View, which leases the farm. For more
information, call (415) 966-6331. It is especially popular with children.
These old nineteenth-century farm buildings were built by the Grant
brothers, who purchased the land in 1860 for cattle ranching.

This is one of the few parks in the low foothills on the east side
of the range. With an elevation ranging from 400 to over 1,400 feet,
this area is characterized by chaparral and grasslands and by oak woodlands composed of several species of oak, bay, madrone, and buckeye.
Wildflowers cover the grassy hillsides in early spring. The oaks here are
excellent for climbing, and a rest stop in the shade of their sprawling
limbs may help you appreciate why the Druids of ancient Gaul and
Britain considered oak forests to be the most sacred of places.

The park is managed to provide a balance between recreational
and agricultural use. A working farm remains on the property and cattle
graze on the grasslands. But they don't seem to bother the yellow
meadowlark or deter the black-tail deer, which are common here. You
may also see piles of sticks, resembling beaver hutches, which are the
home of dusky-footed woodrats. Most of the Park's trails are old ranch
roads which may be explored by foot, horse, or bicycle.

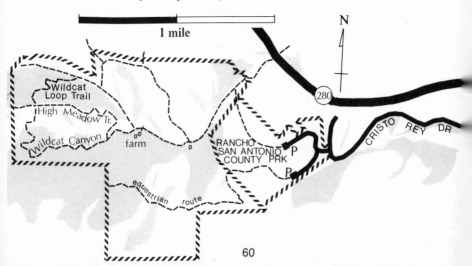

The animals at Deer Hollow Farm help to make Rancho San Antonio one of the most popular open space preserves.

Rancho San Antonio Open Space can be linked with Duveneck Windmill Pasture Open Space to the west; and from there, up the hill to Monte Bello and on to the "Skyline-to-the-Sea" trail. The route to Duveneck makes a moderate 4-6 mile walk each way, depending on the trails. The land between the two parks, however, is private, and the Midpeninsula Regional Open Space District doesn't encourage walking here. These routes are not blocked, though, and hikers have been crossing them for years.

The least objectionable route is through the Kaiser Cement property via the power lines connecting the Black Mountain Trail. A Kaiser spokesman told me his company has no objection to people taking this route as long as they stay on the trails. In order to preserve access, please respect property rights.

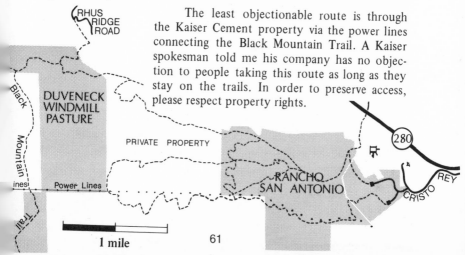

Russian Ridge Open Space

TO GET THERE . . . from Highway 280 take Page Mill Road uphill and west to where it intersects Skyline Boulevard. The preserve begins at the northwest corner of the intersection. Another access is at the vista point turnoff on Skyline a little over a mile to the north.

This high and grassy promontory is perfect for an easy casual saunter. Don't let the absence of formal trails deter you. This is a place to explore; replete with lots of unconnected cow trails and the faint traces of ranch roads that make ideal footpaths.

If you don't like what passes here for trails, blaze your own. Head out footloose over the grassy slopes, exploring the bay, oak, and buckeye groves that are neatly creased into the folds of the ridge; but try not to stray onto private lands bordering the preserve. Remember, if you have to climb through or over a barbed wire fence, you are probably trespassing.

For a more structured ramble, walk the old ranch road on the spine of the ridge. It can be reached by ascending the hill at the southern access or by entering the dirt road gate entrance at the vista point and heading uphill. This route offers an overview of the whole preserve, visiting the highest points and unfolding a 360-degree panoramic display of Mount Tamalpais and San Francisco to the north; the bay and Mount Diablo to the east; Mount Umunhum and Monterey Bay to the south; and the ocean to the west.

This is an outstanding place to see wildflowers in the Spring. After a winter rain I found enormous spherical mushrooms more than a foot in diameter on a boulder-crowned promontory, looking very much like boulders themselves. This is also an ideal place for skiing on those rare winter days when snow mantles the hills. With its smooth, rounded forms, Russian Ridge offers miles of cross-country skiing — and some surprisingly good downhill runs too. Keep your skis ready at a moment's notice between December and February. Conditions may only be good for a few hours, usually in the early morning.

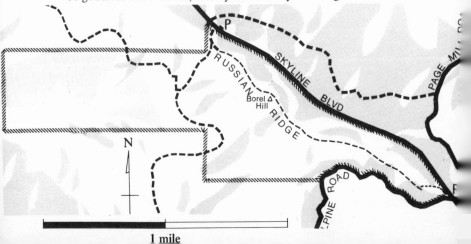

1 mile

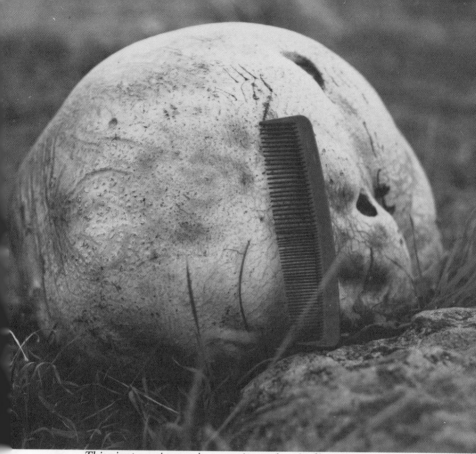

This giant mushroom is more than a foot in diameter.

Sam McDonald County Park

TO GET THERE. . .take La Honda-Pescadero Road about 3 miles west of La Honda.

This is a beautiful 860 acres of redwoods and an ideal destination for a picnic and a hike. The park is kept in a semi-primitive state by limiting automobile access only to the park office area off Pescadero Road. Three walk-in campgrounds, available by reservation, range in distance from .5 to about 1 mile from the parking lot.

The McDonald Trail loop is a good 3.1 mile hike northwest from the parking lot, and though not very long, this peaceful redwood garden of sorrel and ferns has plenty of scenic diversions and its share of challenging ups and downs. The continuation of the McDonald Trail beginning on the other side of the parking lot is equally rewarding. This part of the trail continues as a dirt road for about 2 miles southwest from Pescadero Road and passes some splendid first-growth redwoods, the most magnificent of which can be seen along the short footpath that crosses and then returns back to the dirt road. The route climbs the steep hillside to the top of the ridge, where redwoods give way to grassy areas and oak trees.

Campers who prefer an artificial sky to the real one may want to stay in the Sierra Club's hikers hut on the ridge about a mile from the

parking lot. This small structure, which was shipped from Denmark in prefabricated pieces, has an electric stove, water, a sleeping area, and an aerobic decay toilet. This is the first of what some people hope will be a series of shelters along the expanding trail system between the bay and the ocean. For more information and reservations, call the Sierra Club at (415) 327-8111.

Sam McDonald's southern boundary touches Pescadero Creek County Park which is reached by fire trail. From there it is possible to hike to Portola State Park and San Mateo Memorial Park.

This is one of the greenest and most densely forested of the redwood parks, but it is almost deserted during the winter months. The area was logged early in this century, but some of the grand old big trees survived.

Backpackers should consider hiking fire trails from Sam McDonald to Pescadero Creek and San Mateo Memorial county parks and Portola State Park. The hike is about 4.5 miles from Sam McDonald Park headquarters to the trail along Pescadero Creek which connects San Mateo Memorial and Portola Parks. The total distance to San Mateo Memorial County Park is about 6 miles, and to Portola State Park is a little more than 7 miles. This is a beautifully scenic trail that climbs past first and second-growth redwoods to grassy hilltop vistas and then descends into a forest of Douglas fir and second-growth redwoods. When you get to the top of the ridge, in the grassy meadow, head east on the intersecting ridge trail and continue until the road forks in 3 directions. Take the middle road and stay to the right until it crosses Pescadero Creek and intersects the fire road paralleling the creek. An alternative route back to the parking lot can be taken from here by heading west and north on the ridgetop dirt road, crossing Pescadero Road and hiking southeast by footpath.

Sam McDonald (1884-1957) was a popular Stanford University employee who owned the property until his death. He loved nature and willed that his forest be preserved in its natural state. Stanford owned the land until it became a county park in 1969.

For more information and reservations for group camping, call park headquarters at (415) 747-0403.

Heritage Grove

This 37-acre, old-growth redwood grove adjoins Sam McDonald Park and can be reached by trail from the hikers' hut or by traveling east on Alpine Road one mile from its intersection with Pescadero Road. This magnificent grove was scheduled to be logged until a citizens group raised funds and purchased the land. The loggers' paint marks can still be seen on some of the trees they intended to remove. Several short nature trails make this a wonderful stroll through the redwoods.

SEE MAP ON PAGE 58

San Bruno Mountain County Park

TO GET THERE. . .take Bayshore Boulevard in Brisbane, turn west on Guadalupe Road, and south on Radio Road to the ridgetop.

This 1,314 foot high promontory is a grassland island in an urban sea and is the only large open space in this densely settled and industrialized area. It's an ecological remnant of northern San Mateo County and a wonderful wildflower garden in spring. Actually, this "mountain" consists of 2 parallel ridges separated by the Guadalupe Valley.

To explore the mountain, walk east on the Ridge Trail from the parking lot near the radio towers. This path offers at least 3 miles of walking round trip. Another trail system to the west, starting at Radio Road, forms a scenic and moderately easy 3-mile loop, with lots of views of the great urban expanses of San Francisco to the north, and South San Francisco and Daly City to the south.

This 2,000-acre park is home to at least 384 native plants and 2 rare butterflies. The Mission blue butterfly, already on the endangered species list, and the San Francisco silverspot, proposed for endangered species status, live here and have caused quite a controversy over housing development in the area. A compromise was reached when a major housing developer modified his design to ensure that there would be room for both people and butterflies.

Most of the mountain is covered with coastal scrub vegetation and with annual grasses that make it green in the winter and spring and golden brown in summer. Most of the trees are in the canyons and on north-facing slopes. A few coastal wood, bracken, and chain ferns dwell in moist and shady places.

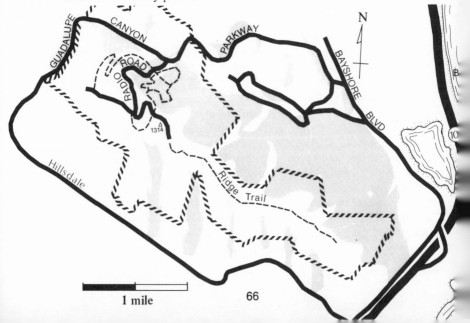

San Mateo County Memorial Park

TO GET THERE. . .it's southwest of Sam McDonald Park on Pescadero Road.

Visitors to San Mateo County Memorial Park may swim in Pescadero Creek, camp, picnic, and hike about 5 miles of trails. The park covers about 350 acres and has lots of beautiful redwoods and some interesting trails, though none of them are long enough to contain the enthusiasm of a good hiker. The Mount Ellen-Summit Trail-Lower Nature Trail loop around the summit of Mount Ellen is a scenic route involving a climb of about 400 feet and a hike of less than 2 miles.

If you're looking for something a bit more challenging than Memorial Park has to offer, try hiking to Portola State Park or Sam McDonald County Park, both about 6 miles away. For information on routes to these parks see the chapters on Pescadero Creek and Sam McDonald county parks.

This park has 140 family campsites, available on a first-come, first-served basis. For more information, call (415) 879-0212.

San Pedro Valley County Park

TO GET THERE. . .take Highway 1 to Pacifica, heading southeast on Linda Mar Boulevard to Oddstad Boulevard. Public parking and park access are next to Saint Peters Catholic Church.

This park is a 1,000 acre mass of coastal scrub and chaparral, with a few grassy places and riperian woodlands for diversity. You can get a look at it by hiking the dirt road along the Middle Fork of San Pedro Creek.

Keep an eye open for the footpath that switchbacks up the hillside from the dirt road, climbing to some nice views of the San Pedro Valley and winding around the hills for 1.6 miles and back to the dirt road. In the spring you will see scrub flowers, and the spicy aroma of sage lingers around the hills all year. Take some time to listen for the mingling melodies of birds.

You may also want to hike the moderate 3-mile South Fork loop trail along the South Fork of San Pedro Creek through riperian and eucalyptus woods and then climb the ridge for a scenic return.

This park has a combination of coastal scrub and true chaparral vegetation, and sometimes it is hard to tell them apart. The main difference is that they each have their own distinct assortment of plants. Both are composed of short, stiff, and thorny vegetation that is virtually impenetrable, which is why this park is not a good place for cross-country hiking. Unfortunately, San Pedro Valley County Park still has relatively few trails and needs a much more extensive trail system

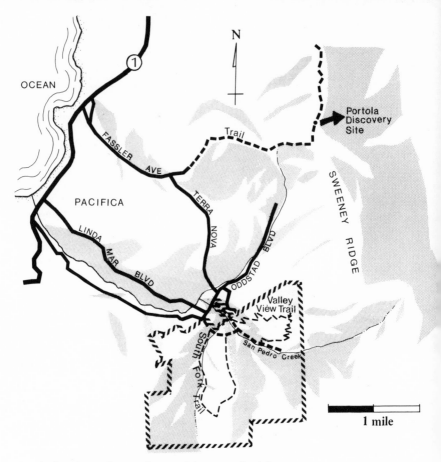

before it can be rated as a prime target for hikers.

The characteristic plant here is coyote brush, a modest shrub with deep roots and small, stiff leaves designed to conserve moisture. It is common along the coast where westerly ocean breezes blow unobstructured. Coyote brush produces small white flowers and has small waxy leaves.

Other common coastal scrub vegetation includes: monkeyflower, shrubby lupine, ceanothus, coastal sage scrub, and thimbleberry. This vegetation thrives in the coastal zone where steady ocean winds sweep the land and make life difficult for most trees. Along the park's small creeks you will notice dense stands of willows, which shelter a ground cover which includes poison hemlock, blackberry vines, horsetails, and bracken ferns.

Sycamores, willows, alders, box elders, and dogwoods are among the streamside trees whose foliage merges together, often covering creeks and making them invisible even from above. Hikers should take note that thorny blackberry vines, fallen tree limbs, and dense tree and shrub growth often make riperian woodlands tough to explore without trails.

There are six species of willows common in this area, the most common of which is the arroyo willow. These beautiful trees have long leaves and produce yellow flowers in the spring. They like the deep, moist soil of streamsides and grow in dense stands that are popular with birds for nesting. They grow as either shrubs or trees and produce tiny seeds which are covered with fluffy cotton-like material. The Ohlone Indians stuck willow sprouts in the ground in circles to form the main supports for their shelters.

This park is open for day use only. For more information, call the park ranger at (415) 359-1881.

The Portola Discovery Site

In the hills above what is now Pacifica, Gaspar de Portola and his haggard expedition discovered San Francisco Bay in November of 1769. The Spanish explorer was too hungry to be impressed, however, and didn't even bother to name the discovery.

Hikers can now make the same trip, though the view has changed quite a bit over the last few centuries. First, stop at the Pacifica City Hall and get a hiking permit. Then drive to the end of Fassler Avenue and hike the 1.8 mile trail uphill about 600 feet to the top of Sweeney Ridge.

The view from the 1,200 foot high ridgetop is spectacular in all directions. The shimmering ocean sprawls out to the west; San Francisco shines to the north like an urban apparition; and Mounts Tamalpais and Diablo puncture the horizon. You will see why Portola wasn't sure if that body of water to the east was a lake or a bay.

Sanborn Skyline County Park

TO GET THERE. . . take Highway 9 (Big Basin Way) west from Saratoga and turn south on Sanborn Road.

Sanborn Skyline County Park covers 2,856 acres on the steep east side of the range and has scenic trails, excellent picnicking facilities, a walk-in campground, and one of the Bay Area's best hostels. From the park's many scenic overlooks you can gaze down on the smoggy haze that often covers San Jose and instead be glad to be in the mountains.

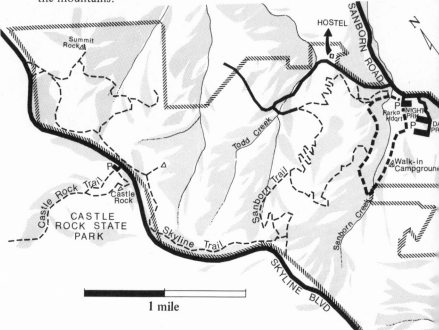

The park has 2 entrances from Sanborn Road, one for day use and another for camping. There are 42 campsites on the Sanborn Trail, available on a first-come, first-served basis. To camp at these sites park at the overnight parking lot, register at the nearby park headquarters, and walk the short distance uphill from the parking lot to the camping area. Each family campsite has a picnic table, a fire place, and restrooms nearby.

Park headquarters are in an interesting sandstone and redwood house built in 1912. Nearby is a self-guided nature trail. The dirt road, which begins at the parking lot, continues uphill past the campground and climbs nearly 1,700 feet in about 3 miles to Skyline Boulevard near the summit of the ridge. This route offers beautiful views of the Santa

The old Welch-Hurst House (1908) has been thoughtfully renovated and is now one of the Bay Area's most attractive and comfortable hostels. It's a wonderful getaway from the city, and a place to meet travelers from around the world.

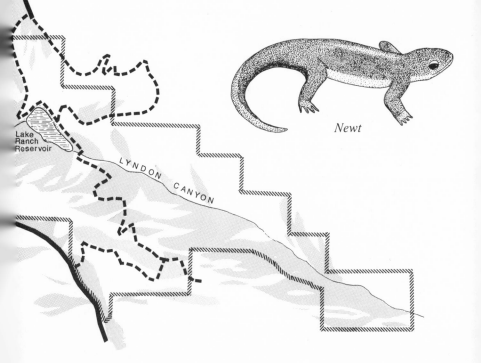

Newt

Lake Ranch Reservoir

LYNDON CANYON

Clara Valley and passes through several different ecological zones. Second-growth redwoods predominate in the shady canyon bottom around park headquarters. Douglas fir, tanoak, bay, and madrone becomes increasingly common in the higher and drier areas where the trail approaches Skyline.

You will probably notice the creeping, climbing wild cucumber plant intertwined with the branches of trees. The Indians used the spiny seed pods of this common vine to cure a variety of ailments, including venereal disease and kidney trouble.

The Sanborn Trail may be used as an extension to the "Skyline-to-the-Sea" trail by parking at the overnight parking lot and hiking west on the Sanborn Trail and north on the Skyline Trail, which connects with Castle Rock State Park. The Castle Rock Trail Camp is an additional 3.2 miles on the Castle Rock Trail, which connects with the "Skyline-to-the-Sea" trail at Saratoga Gap.

The Skyline Trail connects with the Summit Rock Trail which goes to Summit Rock, a sandstone counterpart to Castle Rock and a good place to climb around and explore. It offers a spectacular view of the Santa Clara Valley and has some interesting caves.

This park has one of the most unusual and interesting Youth Hostels in the state. Built of redwood logs, the historic Welch-Hurst House (1908) is about as rustic as anyplace can be, and makes an ideal getaway from the city. Thoughtfully renovated, the inside is comfortable and has many modern conveniences. The log house is in a shadowy grove of redwoods, which also has picnic tables, a barbeque, a wonderful old gazebo, and a duck pond. The Hostel is open all year from 5 p.m. to 9 a.m. For more information, call (415) 867-3993.

Lake Ranch Unit

The southern part of this park can be reached by taking Sanborn Road to its southern end. Though this large area has no formal foot trails as of this writing, it is crossed by an eminently hikable dirt road that climbs to a reservoir and levels out and drops before making a steep assault on the Skyline ridge.

From the end of Sanborn Road take the uphill dirt road to the right. The short, but invigorating ascent to Lake Ranch Reservoir is a great destination for a short ramble. You can stop here and have lunch with the newts, who consider this a favorite hangout. The trail continues around the reservoir and drops a little before climbing to Skyline.

The terrain here is steep and the mountains are wooded with bay, Douglas fir, oak, maple, madrone, and redwood. Just east of the dirt road is the canyon abyss of the San Andreas Fault rift zone, where two continental plates collide.

Except for registered camping, the park is open from 8 a.m. until sundown. For more information, call (408) 867-6940.

Santa Teresa County Park

TO GET THERE . . . take Bernal Road southwest from Highway 101.

Above the south-bounding amorphous sprawl of San Jose, this gentle, grassy park is witness to the dramatic urbanization that is transforming this part of the Santa Clara Valley. Housing tracts and industry sprout at its feet at this narrow part of the valley, making Santa Teresa an important urban recreation area.

Santa Teresa County Park is 1,006 acres of low grassy hills capped by rocky outcroppings which offer views of the Santa Clara Valley immediately below, and Mount Hamilton and the Diablo Range in the distance. The trails here are easy and relaxed; perfect for a picnic. Scattered stands of oak and bay punctuate the grassy hills, which turn brilliant green between January and May, yet are roasted brown by late May as if — as John Muir noted — every leaf and blade had been baked in an oven.

This is also one of the best places around to find miners lettuce. Between February and April great green fields of this delicious leafy herb abound. Bring bowls and salad dressing.

Santa Teresa has excellent equestrian trails, lots of group picnic facilities, a fishing pond, a field archery range, an eighteen-hole golf course, and a field for operating radio-controlled miniature airplanes.

For more information, call the park department at (408) 358-3741.

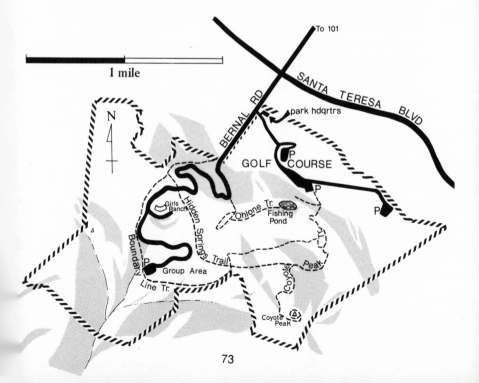

Saratoga Gap Open Space

TO GET THERE . . . the trail through this park can be started at Saratoga Gap near the northeast corner of the intersection of Skyline Boulevard and Highway 9. This trail continues north through Skyline County Park and Monte Bello Open Space.

Saratoga Gap Open Space Preserve is at the northeast corner of Saratoga Gap. The trail through this 492 acre park parallels Skyline Boulevard, crossing grassy hills that explode with wildflowers in early spring. The route then enters 1,165 acre Skyline County Park and dips into the steep, shady canyon that contains the cool and perennial waters of Stevens Creek. You will find many impressive vistas along this trail and see beautiful stands of bay trees, madrone, and canyon live, coast live, and black oak. The Stevens Creek canyon is forested largely with Douglas fir and with big-leaf maple along the creek. The banks of this bouncing, bubbling creek make an excellent picnic stop.

The trail climbs the other slope of the canyon, following a dirt road and rising to the oak and bay studded grasslands of Monte Bello Ridge. Monte Bello Open Space Preserve contains 1,520 acres and can be reached from Saratoga Gap via the trail previously described or from Page Mill Road. The park has a 5 mile trail system on the western slopes of Black Mountain, providing beautiful panoramas, grassy picnicking spots, and amiable old oaks.

There are 3 parks that can be combined to form a grand and diverse hiking adventure of nearly 8 miles from Saratoga Gap to Page Mill Road and Los Trancos Open Space Preserve. Unless you want to hike another 8 miles back, use 2 cars and at least 1 friend and leave a car at Page Mill Road to shuttle back to the trailhead. This hike passes through Saratoga Gap Open Space Preserve, Skyline County Park, and Monte Bello Open Space Preserve. Just north of Page Mill Road is Los Trancos Open Space Preserve. This route explores grassy ridges, chaparral, oak woodlands, and forests of Douglas fir, and involves an elevation range of about 1,400 feet.

Monkey Flower

Manzanita

74

> *"Why preserve open space? Because in the natural world, we find a bond between the past and the future, between our lives and other life. We are humbled and yet exalted, and from that, we find our niche."*

—Kathy Blackburn

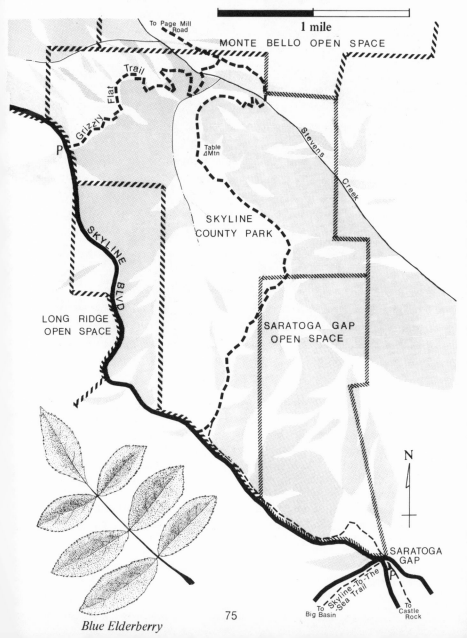

1 mile

To Page Mill Road

MONTE BELLO OPEN SPACE

Grizzly Flat Trail

P

Table △Mtn

Stevens Creek

SKYLINE COUNTY PARK

SKYLINE BLVD

LONG RIDGE OPEN SPACE

SARATOGA GAP OPEN SPACE

N

SARATOGA GAP

P

To Big Basin

Skyline-To-The-Sea Trail

To Castle Rock

Blue Elderberry

This grand old oak is at Skyline Ridge Open Space.

The Santa Cruz Mountains have many noble stands of oak and bay for pursuing the challenging sport of tree climbing. This sport offers all the fun of rock climbing, but with a lot more hand and foot holds and no need for technical aides.

First, you need to know which trees are most climbable. Redwoods and other conifers are usually out of the question because they are too straight and have no low-lying branches. Madrones are sometimes suitable, but their surfaces are usually too smooth to find hand and foot holds.

Oaks of any variety are the best climbing trees, especially those old ones with thick trunks, deep furrowed bark, and large contorted branches that nearly touch the ground. You can climb around like an ape, with never a lack of something to hold on to for support. Bay trees also make great arboreal jungle gyms, and the older and more gnarled the better.

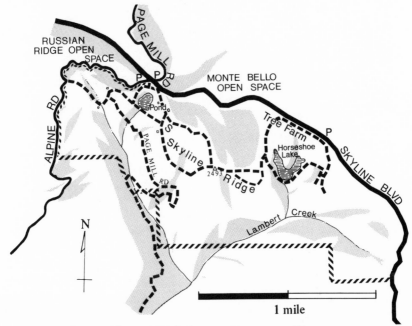

Skyline Ridge Open Space

TO GET THERE ... from Highway 280 take Page Mill Road uphill and west to where it intersects Skyline Boulevard and turns into Alpine Road. The preserve begins at the southwest corner of the intersection. Another access is at the gate to the Christmas tree farm about a mile south of the Alpine/Skyline intersection.

This is a walkers' paradise, with an excellent ranch road trail system that passes by several beautiful reservoirs, wanders through shady forests, and climbs high, scenic ridgetops.

A few of the major trails are on the map; but there are many other paths that fit together into a nearly infinite combination of possible routes. The best advice is to go there and walk. Explore the pond at the Alpine/Skyline access, and turn right (west) for a gradual downhill ramble through oak, madrone, and Douglas fir woodlands. The original Page Mill Road west of Skyline, built in the nineteenth century for hauling redwood lumber, runs through here as a dirt road.

For a more uplifting walk, head left (east) and take the ranch road uphill to the highest point in the preserve at 2,493 feet. The view into the steep canyon below is truly breathtaking. Continuing east, you will walk by contorted old oaks, and through grassy fields and neat rows of Christmas trees.

One of the best things about the southeast part of the preserve is Horseshoe Lake, probably named because of its shape. This is a good sized body of water; large enough for canoeing. There might even be a few fish in there too.

The easiest entry into this part of the preserve is at a gate into the

Christmas tree farm, on Skyline just over a mile south of Alpine Road. Though the land is being cultivated by private tree farmers who lease 123 acres, this is still public parkland; so walk right through. Take one of the dirt road trails down to Horsehoe Lake. Just west of the lake an intersecting trail veers to the south and climbs past another Christmas tree grove and uphill further to the splendid panorama at the highest point in the preserve. From here you can see thousands of feet down into the Peters Creek canyon to the west; Loma Prieta, the highest peak in the range, to the south; and Monte Bello Ridge and Mount Diablo to the east.

This 841 acre preserve is an important part of the Skyline open space corridor, and will be a key link in the developing Skyline Corridor Trail through San Mateo and Santa Clara counties. This park is part of more than 7,500 acres of contiguous open space and parkland on the Skyline Ridge area. For more information, call the Midpeninsula Regional Open Space District (415) 965-4717.

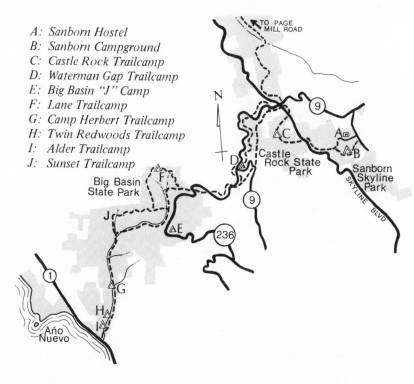

A: Sanborn Hostel
B: Sanborn Campground
C: Castle Rock Trailcamp
D: Waterman Gap Trailcamp
E: Big Basin "J" Camp
F: Lane Trailcamp
G: Camp Herbert Trailcamp
H: Twin Redwoods Trailcamp
I: Alder Trailcamp
J: Sunset Trailcamp

The "Skyline-to-the-Sea" Trail

TO GET THERE ... the trail begins at the intersection of Skyline and Highway 9, or at Highway 1 at Waddell Creek. It can be extended through Castle Rock State Park, Sanborn Skyline County Park, and Monte Bello open space.

Skyline to Big Basin

The "Skyline-to-the-Sea" trail gives hikers a chance to do some real backpacking from Saratoga Gap or Castle Rock State Park to Big Basin Redwoods State Park and on to the coast.

The total distance from Saratoga Gap to the ocean is about 28 miles. The trail passes through grasslands, chaparral, and forests of oak, madrone, Douglas fir and redwoods, and impressive vistas are common along the route.

The trailhead at Saratoga Gap (where Skyline Boulevard intersects Highway 9) is on the south side of Highway 9 just west of Skyline. From the Castle Rock State Park trailcamp the trail crosses Skyline twice before connecting the main trail at Saratoga Gap. The trail parallels Highway 9 for about 8 miles from Saratoga Gap to Waterman Gap campground. The distance to Waterman Gap from the Castle Rock trailhead is about 15.5 miles.

The "Skyline-to-the-Sea" trail, which was built by thousands of volunteers in 1969, closely parallels highways 9 and 236 because this land was already owned by the state. Hikers who prefer straying farther from the sound of traffic should try hiking the Toll Road south of Highway 9. This abandoned logging road, built in 1870, connects with the main "Skyline-to-the-Sea" route west of Saratoga Gap and again west of the junction of Highways 9 and 236. Because this route may be hard to follow, a topographic map and compass may come in handy to avoid getting lost. As of this writing the public right of way for parts of this route is being challenged by local property owners and its legal status may change in the near future. This is an example of the need for hikers to become politically active to defend our trails.

The trail continues for about 9.5 miles from Waterman Gap to Big Basin Park Headquarters. Take the Soroptimist-Opal Creek Trail from China Grade. Hikers should be aware that starting the trail at Castle Rock adds 7.5 miles to the total distance to Big Basin. From China Grade Road the trail passes through chaparral and stands of knobcone pine and enters the shady redwood groves along Opal Creek. Just before the trail drops into Big Basin you will be greeted by splendid views of the mountains to the southwest, and on clear days you may also get a glimpse of the ocean.

Due to a lack of water on parts of the trail during the dry season, hikers are advised to bring water. The Castle Rock campground has water, pit toilets, and fireplaces. The Waterman Gap campground has water, pit toilets, and does not permit ground fires. The Big Basin "J" camp has water, flush toilets, fireplaces, and showers. Campsite reservations may be made in person, by phone, or by mail up to 90 days in advance at Big Basin. Call (408) 338-6132.

Big Basin to the Sea

The new "Big Basin-to-the-Sea" trail follows Waddell Creek through the 1,700 acre "Rancho Del Oso" property, which connects the state park with the coast. This trail can be found by taking the Berry Creek Falls Trail to near the confluence of Waddell and Berry creeks, and by following Waddell Creek downstream. The distance from park headquarters to Highway 1 is about 10.5 miles on the Berry Creek Falls Trail, about 11 miles on the Howard King Trail, and about 12 miles on the Sunset Trail. The Berry Creek Trail has the easiest grade of these three routes. Hikers taking the Sunset Trail may want to make camp at the Sunset Trailcamp, which is about a quarter mile east of Berry Creek and upstream from Golden Falls.

There are 3 trailcamps in "Rancho Del Oso": Camp Herbert is about 7.5 miles from Big Basin park headquarters; Twin Redwoods is 1.5 miles downstream from Camp Herbert; and Alder Camp is less than a mile downstream from Alder Camp. Ground fires are prohibited and campers are encouraged to make reservations by calling Big Basin park headquarters at (408) 338-6132.

Racoons are a common delight, but they can be a problem for backpackers. Usually nocturnal, they eat almost anything they can get their little paws on, including your food. If you're bothered by hungry racoons at night, throw a rope over a tree branch and hoist your food out of their reach.

This beautiful canyon was an ideal place for the Ohlone Indians, who gathered marine edibles from the coast and stalked game in the mountains. Mammals you may see here include coyotes, racoons, deer, bobcats, foxes, weasels, possums, skunks, several species of squirrels, chipmunks, and an assortment of other rodents. Bears no longer roam these mountains and mountain lions are rare. This is still an important feeding and nesting area for birds, with more than 200 species sighted. Near the trail is the Eagle Tree, an impressive first-growth redwood which once hosted an eagle nest.

The old "Big Basin-to-the-Sea" trail may still be used by taking the Sunset Trail to the Sunset trailcamp and west to a ridgetop fire road and to the coast on Whitehouse Road. Sunset camp is 5.5 miles from park headquarters and has water, pit toilets, and does not permit ground fires.

A detailed topographic map of the entire "Skyline-to-the-Sea" trail is available by sending a self-addressed, stamped envelope and 35 cents to Sempervirens Fund, P.O. Box 1141, Los Altos, California 94022.

The "Skyline-to-the-Sea" trail is the hub of a vast network of trails developing in this part of the Santa Cruz Mountains. It is now possible to hike about 8.5 miles from Los Trancos Open Space Preserve on Page Mill Road to Saratoga Gap, where you can connect with the "Skyline-to-the-Sea" trail. To hike from one side of the range to the other, park at Sanborn-Skyline County Park and take the Sanborn and Skyline trails to Castle Rock State Park and on to Saratoga Gap via the Castle Rock Trail.

A new trail is now being built between Big Basin and Portola state parks. The Olmo Fire Trail goes from Butano State Park to the China Grade Road in Big Basin, though public access to this route is still disputed. See the appropriate chapters for more detailed information on these connecting trails.

See the Big Basin and Castle Rock chapters for more detailed maps and information.

Tourists at Big Basin in the 1920s.

Conservationists have been active in the Santa Cruz Mountains since the beginning of this century, when San Jose photographer Andrew P. Hill (1853-1922) started a movement to establish California's first state park at Big Basin in 1901. Angered by unrestricted logging, he founded the Sempervirens Club to protect the outstanding natural beauty of the area.

Hill's work continues today as the Sempervirens Fund, a non-profit organization which raises funds for the completion of Castle Rock and Big Basin state parks. They also help to build trails and plant trees in the two parks. To participate, write to: Sempervirens Fund, P.O. Box 1141, Los Altos, California 94022.

Uvas Canyon County Park

TO GET THERE. . . take Croy Road west from Uvas Road. It's west of Morgan Hill.

This 1,049-acre wooded park is tucked into a beautiful canyon west of Morgan Hill. Here you can escape the crowds and hike about 7 miles of trails along shady creeks and through wonderfully diverse forests of second-growth redwood, Douglas fir, bay, madrone, sycamore, bigleaf maple, buckeye, and several kinds of oak.

A great day hike can be taken on the loop trail beginning at the "nature trail" about a quarter mile beyond the bridge on the left side of the road. Follow the Swanson Creek Trail until it crosses Swanson Creek beyond the Old Hot House Site. This part of the route becomes the Contour Trail, which gains elevation and eventually intersects Alec Canyon Trail. Turn left here and return to the starting point. This loop is only about 3 easy miles and involves just a little uphill hiking. Short sidetrips from the loop trail can be made to Black Rock Falls and Basin Falls.

For a more vigorous walk, climb Nibbs Knob by way of the Nibbs Knob Fire Trail. This 3-mile round trip climbs more than 1,400 feet for a commanding panorama of the region.

The park has a family campground, available on a first-come, first-serve basis, and picnic facilities. For more information, call (408) 779-9232.

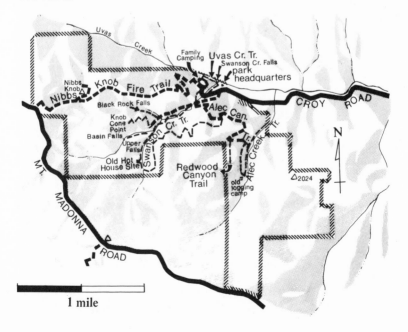

83

Villa Montalvo Arboretum

TO GET THERE... take Saratoga-Los Gatos Road south of Highway 9 in Saratoga and turn southwest on Montalvo Road.

Villa Montalvo is a 175 acre cultural center, arboretum, and wildlife refuge in the hills west of Saratoga. The mansion is maintained by the Montalvo Association, and the remainder of the grounds have been under Santa Clara County jurisdiction since 1960.

Villa Montalvo is a very unique park. Because it is more of an educational than a recreational facility, there are no picnicking or camping facilities available. An easy 1.5 mile self-guided nature loop climbs about 400 feet into the Santa Cruz Mountains foothills. The park has only about 3 miles of trails, making it a good place for casual hikes and an excellent place to study the ecology of the east side of the Santa Cruz Mountains.

You can tell a lot about an area by the relationship between grasslands and oak trees. Oaks don't die out during the summer dry spell as do the annual grasses, and though they have deeper roots than the grasses, they need a lot more moisture to survive. A dense stand of oaks is an indication of available ground water, while a wide spacing of trees tells us that underground water is scarce and must be conserved among trees.

The arboretum is open to the public from 8 a.m. to 5 p.m. and the mansion is open from 1 p.m. to 4 p.m. The grounds and mansion were bought by California Senator and San Francisco Mayor James Phelan in 1911. Rooms on the estate are now rented to promising artists.

For more information, call (408) 867-0190.

Windy Hill Open Space

TO GET THERE ... take Skyline Boulevard 5 miles north of the Page Mill intersection and 2.3 miles south of the Woodside Road intersection. Park at the picnic area on the east side of Skyline.

If ever a hill lived up to its name this is it. In fact, Windy Hill Open Space Preserve is a whole area of high, grassy hills, seen from much of the Bay Area, and exposed to the currents of wind that wash over the Santa Cruz Mountains from the sea. Without a formal trail system, but with a whole network of unofficial footpaths and old ranch roads, this is a wonderful land for a lighthearted romp, a picnic, and especially for kite flying.

Take the foot trail from the picnic table area to the slope of Windy Hill itself and make a hardy ascent to the top. Here you will

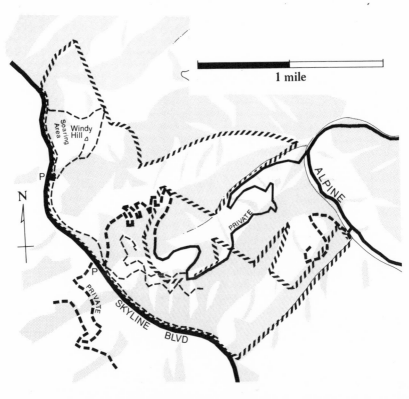

The view from Windy Hill.

find one of the Santa Cruz Mountains' great views, with the bay and its cities spread out below. This windswept point is perfect for kite flying, with no entangling trees or telephone wires.

If you grow tired of the wind, follow the footpath as it contours the hill and descends to a quiet and shady little grove of Monterey Cypress. The western slopes of Windy Hill have been designated a soaring area, for use by non-motorized model gliders. For more information, write: South Bay Soaring Society, P.O. Box 2012, Sunnyvale, CA 94087.

The southern part of the preserve is largely covered with chaparral, and madrone, bay, and Douglas fir woodlands. To explore this area, walk or drive just under a mile from the picnic area to the gate at the dirt road that intersects Skyline. Either walk on the maintained dirt road, or turn south just beyond the gate on the deteriorated old ranch roads.

Windy Hill was donated to the Midpeninsula Regional Open Space District with the help of the Peninsula Open Space Trust, which works with private landowners for protecting baylands, the San Mateo County coast, and the Skyline scenic corridor.

Wunderlich County Park

TO GET THERE... take Woodside Road west from Interstate 280. Turn in at the parking lot at 4040 Woodside Road, about 2 miles southwest of the town of Woodside.

This is one of the most ecologically diverse and scenically beautiful parks east of Skyline. It's well used by equestrians, but there are surprisingly few hikers enjoying the park's 942 acres.

From the park entrance parking lot, at the Folger Ranch buildings, this looks like an oakwood-brushland park. But a hike up the hillside reveals dark, cool groves of second-growth redwoods, open grassy meadows, and nearly pure stands of Douglas fir. This is a steep park, with an elevation range of more than 1,650 feet; but it has excellent trails that are graded to avoid excessively strenuous climbs.

A beautiful half day, 4.75 mile (7.6 kilometers), hike can be taken by combining the Bear Gulch and Alambique trails. From the parking lot hike uphill on Bear Gulch Trail, passing through live oak groves and pockets of redwoods in shady creek beds.

Along the trail stands the rotting remains of a fence built when Simon Jones owned the property in the latter part of the last century. You will also find a long trough running up the hill. This is one of several skid trails created by oxen dragging redwood logs down the mountain between about 1850 and 1865 to provide lumber for Bay Area cities. The forest has re-grown, but this furrow will probably remain for centuries. You will also see large Douglas fir trees with low, sprawling branches, indicating that at one time these trees were in open meadowland which was overgrown with trees when cattle grazing ceased.

Suddenly the forests give way to a beautiful meadow, covered with native bunch grasses and introduced perennials. Around the edges of this grassland stand large climbable oaks, and there are sweeping views that make this a great place to stop and relax for awhile.

The Alambique Trail heads downhill, through all the park's native plant communities, and passing such introduced species as Monterey cyprus, eucalyptus, and olive trees. Be sure to pause and admire the enormous first-growth redwood on the north side of the trail — the kind you wouldn't expect to see east of Skyline. You will also see the ruins of old nineteenth century wagon bridges along the way.

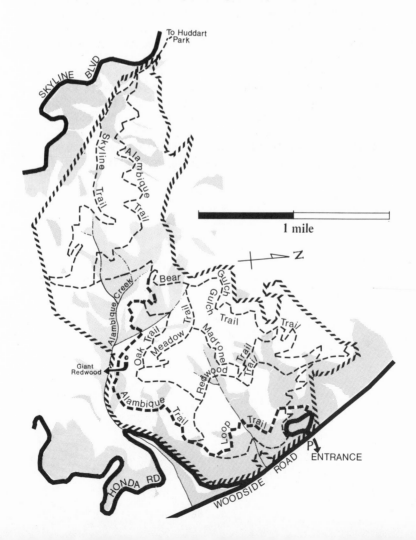

If you have all day or more than the usual amount of energy, hike the 5 mile (8 kilometers) round trip from the meadows to Skyline and back. From Bear Gulch Trail, hike uphill on Alambique Trail to the top of the ridge and then gambol down the Skyline Trail and back to Alambique Creek, which flows along the course of a branch of Pilarcitos Fault. Notice that the rock suddenly changes from sandstone to shale as you cross the fault. Also notice that Douglas fir increasingly forests the steep hillside as you climb towards the Skyline ridge.

This park has an exceptional abundance and variety of poison oak. Few people ever stop to appreciate the changing beauty of the poison oak plant. In autumn it changes from bright green to a brilliant red, and in spring it forms little cream-colored flowers. It's sometimes hard to identify because it can grow as either a shrub or a vine. Those of us who are immune to the plant's poison have the luxury of enjoying its unusual charm. The rest of you should learn to recognize it in all its forms and give it a wide berth.

Hikers should be aware that this park is heavily used for horse riding and that it is sometimes necessary to watch where you are stepping. You should also be warned that all the trail signs have distances listed in metric units. Remember, there are 1.609 kilometers to a mile.

This park is open for day use only. For more information, call the San Mateo County Parks Department at (415) 364-5600.

See page 47 for details on the Skyline Trail to Huddart Park.

Organizations and Agencies

There's a lot happening in the Santa Cruz Mountains: walking, backpacking, nature study, trail building, and conservation activities. Here are some of the private and governmental organizations and agencies you may want to contact.

Año Nuevo Interpretive Association: (Nature education); 95 Kelly Ave., Half Moon Bay, CA 94019; (415) 726-6238.

Audubon Society: (outings and conservation activities); Santa Clara Valley Chapter: 2253 Park Blvd., Palo Alto, CA 94306; (415) 328-5315; Sequoia Chapter: 6736 Mission, Daly City, CA 94014; (415) 755-3221.

California State Parks Department: (Santa Cruz Mountains regional office); Henry Cowell Redwoods State Park, Felton, CA 95018; (408) 335-5858.

Committee For Green Foothills: (Conservation); 2253 Park Blvd., Palo Alto, CA 94306; (415) 328-5313.

Hidden Villa Association: (Environmental education and hostel); 26870 Moody Rd., Los Altos Hills, CA 94022; Environmental education: (415) 941-6119; Hostel: (415) 941-6407.

Midpeninsula Regional Open Space District: (Docent walks and information); 375 Distel Circle, Los Altos, CA 94022; (415) 965-4717.

Mountain View Parks Department: (Deer Hollow Farm); 201 S. Rengstorff Ave., Mountain View, CA 94040; (415) 966-6331.

Nature Explorations: (Walks and nature study); 2253 Park Blvd., Palo Alto, CA 94306; (415) 324-8737.

Peninsula Conservation Center: (Conservation activities and environmental library); 2253 Park Blvd., Palo Alto, CA 94306; (415) 328-5313.

Peninsula Open Space Trust: (Acquisition and protection of open space); 3000 Sand Hill Rd., Menlo Park, CA 94025; (415) 854-7696.

San Mateo County Parks Department: County Office Building, Redwood City, CA 94063; (415) 363-4021.

Santa Clara County Parks Department: 298 Garden Hill Dr., Los Gatos, CA 95030; (408) 356-7151.

The Santa Cruz Mountains Natural History Association: P.O. Box P-1, Felton, CA 95018; (408) 335-5858.

The Santa Cruz Mountains Trail Association: (Trail building and maintenance); P.O. Box 1141, Los Altos, CA 94022.

Sempervirens Fund: (Parkland acquisition and trail building); P.O. Box 1141, Los Altos, CA 94022; (415) 968-4509.

Sierra Club: (Outings and conservation activities); Loma Prieta chapter: 2253 Park Blvd., Palo Alto, CA 94306; (415) 327-8111.

Santa Cruz Mountains' Trees

MONTEREY CYPRESS
Grows mainly along coast.

DOUGLAS FIR
One of the most common trees
in the range.

KNOBCONE PINE
Found on dry, rocky ridgetops.

CALIFORNIA NUTMEG
Stiff, sharp needles.

REDWOOD
Flourishes in moist canyon
bottoms. Found mostly on
the west side of the range.

CALIFORNIA BLACK OAK
Often found on ridges on the
east side of the range.

BLUE OAK
Grows on the dry east side of
the mountain.

COAST LIVE OAK
Drought resistant. Common on
dry hillsides.

INTERIOR LIVE OAK
Grows as a shrub with
chaparral or as a tree on
wooded hillsides.

TANOAK
Often grows on ridges and
mixed with redwood and
Douglas fir.

CALIFORNIA WHITE OAK
Common at low elevations east
of Skyline.

OREGON WHITE OAK
Found mostly on dry ridges.

RED ALDER
Riperian tree.

OREGON ASH

BAY TREE
Common on the east side of
the range. Leaves are fragrant
and used for seasoning.

BLUEBLOSSOM
Grows in moist, wooded areas.

BLUE ELDERBERRY
Found mostly on the east side
of the range. Often grows with
chaparral.

BOXELDER
Found on low hills and creekbeds.

CALIFORNIA BUCKEYE
Common on east side of the
range. Leaves drop in summer
and reappear in February.

CHRISTMASBERRY TOYON
Common in dry areas. Red
berries appear in winter.

BLACK COTTONWOOD
Found in streamside wood-
lands.

EUCALYPTUS
Large non-native tree. Prefers
low elevations.

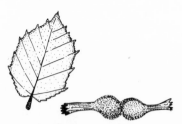

PACIFIC DOGWOOD
Grows along creeks.

CALIFORNIA HAZEL
Small understory tree. Shade tolerant.

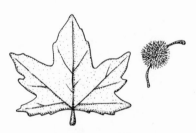

MADRONE
Common on dry ridges. Bark peels.

BIGLEAF MAPLE
Loses leaves in late fall.

WAX MYRTLE
A small coastal creekside tree.

CALIFORNIA SYCAMORE
Found mostly near creeks.

ARROYO WILLOW
Common streamside tree.

HINDS WALNUT

A native of the Bay Area, Tom Taber has been exploring the Santa Cruz Mountains nearly as long as he has been able to walk. He has also done extensive backpacking and day hiking in the Sierra, the Big Sur area, the North Coast, Death Valley, and the Trinity Alps. He has also explored Europe, Central America, and Alaska.

Tom's other interests include river rafting, wildlife study, photography, and self publishing. He is a graduate of the University of California at Davis and works in the graphic arts field. His other books are: FROM BODEGA BAY TO MONTEREY (1977), and DISCOVERING SAN FRANCISCO BAY (1978).